THE HEART OF RECOGNITION

THE HEART OF RECOGNITION
THE WISDOM & PRACTICES OF THE PRATYABHIJNA HRDAYAM

Swami Khecaranatha

Sutras Translated by Keith Jefferds

Also by Swami Khecaranatha

Depth Over Time: Kundalini MahaYoga:
A Path of Transformation and Liberation
(Author House, 2010)

Merging With the Divine: One Day at a Time
(Prasad Press, 2012)

Shiva's Trident: The Consciousness of Freedom
and The Means to Liberation (forthcoming in 2013)

All books and audio/video recordings, including several guided meditations, are available online and may be ordered from SwamiKhecaranatha.com.

Swami Khecaranatha's books are published under his own imprint, Prasad Press.

Dedication

I dedicate this book to my partner Sonia,
a cherished treasure in my life.

Acknowledgments

This book is the result of the work of a team of people whose many talents have brought it to published form. I am grateful for their assistance and wish to extend my thanks to all of them.

Breda Boran-Sears performed the arduous task of transcribing many of the talks from my retreats to create a raw manuscript.

Ellen Jefferds served as editor for the book and took primary responsibility for creating and implementing the layout.

Sonia Foscoli, Sassi LaMuth, and Christine Sheridan read the manuscript and provided invaluable feedback that helped bring clarity and flow to the content.

Christine also took on the painstaking work of copyediting the final manuscript.

Keith Jefferds translated the Sanskrit text, created the tattvas chart, and helped design the cover.

Translator's Note

Savants of a good sutra know it to be of few words,
unambiguous, pithy, comprehensive, unhesitant,
unimpeachable.

While this traditional definition of a sutra (which is itself a sutra!) might bring to mind the instructions in a well-written computer manual, the demands of composing sutras were far more exacting than for any technical writer—and the importance of "getting it right" was infinitely more vital to the life of the "end user." Just like a poet or novelist, the sutra writer had to dig deep to hone his or her message; the goal, however, was not individual self-expression but the exacting precision that springs from consummate knowledge, a rigorous conciseness that could capture in essence the entire theoretical underpinnings of an established science, practice, discipline, or even, as in the case of the *Pratyabhijna Hrdayam*, the wholeness of creation and its source.

In Sanskrit, sutra means "thread," and the word is in fact cognate—that is, related in its origin—with our own "sew" and "suture." As a technical term, sutra may at first have been used quite literally: sutras were aphoristic guides, palm-leaf manuscripts bound together by threads. The word acquired a much greater figurative sense when collected sutras or verses were seen as the very threads on which hung the whole fabric of a particular teaching. To carry through with this metaphor, we might say that sutras hold together the mantle of knowledge that a student (who, by tradition, memorizes the sutras of his or her particular discipline) may finally come to wear. In a sense, the "garment" of the teaching brings out the beauty of the student, while the student grows into and fills out the garment.

It is often noted that in order to translate a work of poetry, fiction, or drama, the translator must be not only a confident linguist and cultural historian but an artist as well—able in some sense to rewrite the work, preserving the original spirit and intent while clothing it in fresh rhythms, sounds, and idioms that help new readers access that spirit. Translating sutras is an entirely different proposition. The same burden of precision and knowledge taken up by the original writer must also be carried by the translator. But as all students of Sanskrit know, even English, with its vast and rich vocabulary, can be a limiting medium in the translation of Sanskrit, an ancient language that resonates with metaphoric and technical meanings acquired over thousands of years of continuous culture. There is always a danger of distortion or of imposing preconceptions on the original intent.

Fortunately for translators and students alike, sutras, like other forms of Indian literature, do not come to us in isolation. As they were themselves a distillation, a quintessence of previous knowledge, the sutras in turn became the focus of a centuries-long tradition of detailed commentaries representing the collective insights and experiential verification of countless scholars and teachers. These commentaries are invaluable in revealing the "consensus of insight" surrounding the sutras themselves.

In the case of sutras expounding the nature of reality itself—and the path to living that reality—the greatest resource for a translator is a present master who fully embodies that tradition. I have had the honor and good fortune to work with such a master, Swami Khecaranatha, whose lifelong spiritual practice and in-depth textual study lit my way in translating the twenty sutras of the *Pratyabhijna Hrdayam*. To be precise, I brought the linguistic background and the dictionary; my teacher, Swami Khecaranatha, brought the living Tantra.

Keith Jefferds
Berkeley, California

INTRODUCTION

Introduction

In this book we will be exploring the *Pratyabhijna Hrdayam,* one of the foundational texts of Tantric Shaivism. *Pratyabhijna* means "recognition" and *Hrdayam* means "heart." The word "heart" has a double meaning. It signifies that the text gets to the "heart of the matter" and also that our heart is the center of Life. Our own heart has the capacity to recognize the highest truth in life — that within each of us is the knowledge and experience that we are an individuated expression of the Divine. It is our own inner recognition of this truth that is the core of this teaching. It is literally the "Recognition of the Self."

The *Pratyabhijna Hrdayam* is a very simple, profound, and eloquent text. It comprises twenty *sutras* or aphorisms, a concise way of summarizing a truth. The sutras in the *Pratyabhijna Hrdayam* unfold sequentially, but the discussion of each is vibrant within itself. Each one contains a powerful message that helps us understand our Divine nature and how that same Divinity has manifested and expressed all of life, including ourselves. The text describes the process of Divine Consciousness becoming human consciousness; it then elucidates the unfolding recognition that takes place within human awareness as we experience unity with our Source. In addition, the sutras describe a spiritual practice that provides us the means to discover this nonduality — that there isn't "God" and "us" — there is only God living *as* each of us. This is the central message of this ancient Tantric masterpiece.

Our experience of separation, and the suffering that results from that, stems from our misunderstanding about who is the agent of life. We mistakenly believe that we are the doer. In reality, we are an individuated expression of the unity of life— and much of the discussion in the *Pratyabhijna Hrdayam* is about recognizing that because this is so, everything we do is literally being enacted by that Divine agency. It is a profound teaching because in its essence it says that to recognize your Self, you must surrender yourself. You must surrender all limited experience, all limited understanding, and the self-reinforcing capacity of your own perspective.

This is not a different teaching from what we find in the *Shiva Sutras* or the *Spandakarikas*, which are other foundational Tantric texts. All of them convey essentially the same message but from a slightly different angle. The *Pratyabhijna Hrdayam* was written in the eleventh century by Kshemaraja. He was a student of Abhinavagupta, the great saint who is considered the founder of Tantric Shaivism. Abhinavagupta is the founder in the sense that he consolidated the previous ten centuries of practice of Kundalini Yoga and the philosophical exposition that began to arise in the seventh and eighth centuries. He brought these teachings and practices to a coalescence of clarity that had not been seen before that date and hasn't been seen since.

What is wonderful about the work of Abhinavagupta and Kshemaraja is that after about two thousand years of oral tradition, these teachers decided to write everything down. For them, this knowledge was not just theory. The exposition was the culmination of their experience and that of thousands of truly remarkable people who were inner scientists, who really allowed this understanding to unfold within them.

These sutras are powerful in their simplicity, although they may at times appear to be enigmatic. The obscurity may be intentional because that is how these ancient teachers wrote. They said, "I will give you a glimpse." More importantly, the sutras may seem arcane due to their very simplicity. The authors were writing for an audience of practitioners already established in certain fundamental ideas and experiences—and this text can be seen as a poetic expression of what was already established in that culture.

It's important to understand the relationship between one's personal experience and scriptural texts such as the *Pratyabhijna Hrdayam*. During the first twenty years of my own practice I never opened a spiritual book other than that written by my teacher, Swami Rudrananda (Rudi). He, in turn, was not a reader of scripture or traditional texts. After Rudi passed, I studied for many years with Swami Chetanananda, and we began to study the Tantric tradition in depth. When I started reading the ancient teachings, my initial reaction was that they confirmed my own experience and put it in context. In that sense, my journey has not been different from practitioners like Abhinavagupta and Kshemaraja, who expressed their own direct experience instead of theorizing about the experience of higher consciousness.

What is interesting for us is that these sages *did* document their experiences, and in these twenty sutras they describe the "everything principle." They understood, from within their own awareness, how everything came into being, and, especially important, how we came into being and what we can do to experience our own Source. The discussion can be expressed by the words "a return home," since the recognition of the heart is not creating anything new in us; it is recognizing that which is always present, already within us. This is the beauty of studying the text and the sutras. What I hope to do in this book is help readers understand how the knowledge in the sutras can affect and even determine their own experience.

The masters who write scriptural texts usually start with the highest point, the highest knowledge. They present and argue that highest truth, with supporting discussion, and then at the end the same message is repeated. I find this incredibly wonderful because what these masters are really emphasizing is *this is it*—this is all you need to know. But for those who can't instantly get it from this one opening line, the sages then explain everything again, bit by bit. Finally, after all the complicated exposition—which might confuse as much as clarify—they repeat the highest message.

In all three of the aforementioned classic Tantric texts there are two aspects of the analysis: a discussion about the cosmology of the universe plus an examination of the cosmology of each individual. The crux of the matter is that these are not different or separate. We, as individuated expressions of one Divine whole, go through exactly the same process as the whole Itself. *Pratyabhijna Hrdayam* makes multiple references to these principles, and in a later chapter we will encounter in depth what are called the Fivefold Acts of the Divine—the parallel forms of action that we as individuals share with God.

I will also discuss the thirty-six *tattvas,* which are the Shaivite explanation of how manifest creation emerges from unlimited Consciousness. *Tattva* literally means "that-ness," and the tattvas describe the way in which Consciousness contracts and descends from its universal, undifferentiated state into the lowest level of density—how Shiva becomes "that," without ever losing Himself. This discussion of cosmology is important because it helps us understand both where we fit in the unfolding of creation and how we can transform ourselves so that we merge back into the whole.

The term *Shiva Drishti* translates as, "the supreme viewpoint of Shiva." What we are attempting to do in our spiritual practice is to recognize this viewpoint, to directly experience that "I am Shiva." Of course, we are also Shakti, because Shiva (consciousness) and Shakti (energy) are simply aspects of Unity. Emphasized in the *Pratyabhijna Hrdayam* is that freedom is not just the glimpse of our own Divinity; it is the full merging with that Divinity. The glimpse is part of the Grace that is calling us back home.

Directly expressed within all of these Tantric texts is the practice of Kundalini Yoga, the awakening of the vital force within us. Kundalini penetrates through our psychic body and frees us from all limitation as it rises up the *sushumna*, the central channel, to the center of the head. Through dedicated spiritual practice this experience is available to everyone, as we all have an internal psychic mechanism that can open and unfold the potential within.

The fundamental thing I hope you will take away from this book is a conflicting statement, which is: You are the center and the cause of the universe, yet your life is not about you. We all walk around assured that we are princes and princesses. Furthermore, we walk around pissed off because we haven't been recognized as kings and queens. So we have both arrogance and anger within us. These feelings are a reflection of how we perceive ourselves to be the center of the universe; paradoxically, this diminishes our capacity to recognize that our higher Self *is*, in fact, the center of the universe!

The *Pratyabhijna Hrdayam* describes the experience of Life in the context of our individuality. It presents the Divine perspective that the magnificence of Consciousness is always expressing Itself in Its perfection. It also elucidates why there is no conflict between that highest understanding and our own unfolding experience: that life is not about us, and yet we have the ability to perceive from the Divine perspective. I hope that through the study of the *Pratyabhijna Hrdayam*, you will understand that you have to experience both things. In other words, in order to truly allow that magnificence to express itself in your life, you must first come to the place of total surrender where you realize that your life is not about you.

As we go through our discussion of the *Pratyabhijna Hrdayam*, I will avoid a lot of technical language, including some Sanskrit terms, because that can really get in the way of understanding. Whenever Sanskrit words are used because of their relevance,

I will offer a translation. Because the *Pratyabhijna Hrdayam* is a Shaivite text, the names used for God are Shiva and Shakti. For the sake of simplicity, I often refer to God as "He." However, to move beyond any concept of a personified Shiva and Shakti, or a He and a She, it's also helpful to refer to God as "It." Then, the focus is on Consciousness "Itself," beyond any limitation. The important thing is to understand the nature of Divinity and how It expresses Itself, and not to focus on the terminology.

Finally, nothing in this book is relevant to you, the reader, unless it becomes your experience. For this reason, I will end the discussion of each sutra with a "Recognition," which will summarize my commentary and offer some words about how the knowledge affects our lives. But reading alone is not enough. All the wisdom in the *Pratyabhijna Hrdayam* is someone else's experience if it isn't your own.

THE TWENTY SUTRAS

The Twenty Sutras

ONE

Autonomous Consciousness is the source of the entire universe.

TWO

*Of Its own free will (that Consciousness) unfolds
the universe on the screen of Itself.*

THREE

*It (Consciousness) is diversified by multiplying into
reciprocal subjects and objects.*

FOUR

*Even individuated consciousness, whose essence is Consciousness
in a contracted state, is a contracted form of the universe.*

FIVE

*Unlimited Consciousness, (having further) descended from the
state of individual consciousness, when embodied and contracted
in objects of perception, (becomes) the mind.*

SIX

*One whose nature is that (of mind) perceives maya
(the illusion of separateness).*

SEVEN

And He (the Supreme Consciousness) is one, is dual, is trifold, is fourfold, and consists of seven sets of five.

EIGHT

The premises of all the systems of philosophy are phases of this (the structure of Consciousness).

NINE

That which possesses Consciousness, through contraction of its powers (becomes) a transmigratory individual enveloped in impurities (the veils of duality).

TEN

Even so, the possessor of that (Consciousness) performs the Fivefold Acts (of Shiva).

ELEVEN

These (i.e., the Fivefold Acts of Shiva), take place in the individual as illuminating (the object), fixing our awareness in it, understanding it, (thus) planting a seed (of limitation), and releasing (that misunderstanding).

TWELVE

The state of a transmigratory individual is that of being deceived by one's own powers while failing to recognize that (i.e., the fact of actually being the performer of the Fivefold Acts).

THIRTEEN

When one recognizes that (i.e., being the performer of the Fivefold Acts), the mind itself—by turning within (meditating) and by rising out of the state of limited consciousness—becomes (unlimited) Consciousness.

FOURTEEN

*The fire of Consciousness—though it seems to be in a
descended state—gradually burns up the fuel of the knowable.*

FIFTEEN

*When this (the fire of Consciousness) reaches (full) strength,
the universe becomes one's own.*

SIXTEEN

*On attaining the bliss of Consciousness, there is permanent
perception of oneness with Consciousness even when perceiving
the body and so on. This is liberation while alive.*

SEVENTEEN

*The bliss of Consciousness is revealed through the
unfolding of the center.*

EIGHTEEN

*The means for (the expansion of the center) include attainment
of a thought-free state, expansion of the contracted state
of Shakti (the Power within us), awareness of the beginning
and end points, and stilling of the flow.*

NINETEEN

*Permanent samadhi is established when (all) activity bears the
impression of samadhi through uninterrupted (i.e., repeated,
consistent) experience of oneness with Consciousness.*

TWENTY

*Then, for all time—through absorption in the Self, whose nature
is the power of the Great Mantra and whose essence is the Bliss
of Divine Effulgence—one obtains mastery of the wheel of deities
(energies) that create and withdraw all that is. This is the
auspicious state of Shiva.*

चितिः स्वतन्त्रा विश्वसिद्धिहेतुः

citiḥ svatantrā viśvasiddhihetuḥ

SUTRA ONE

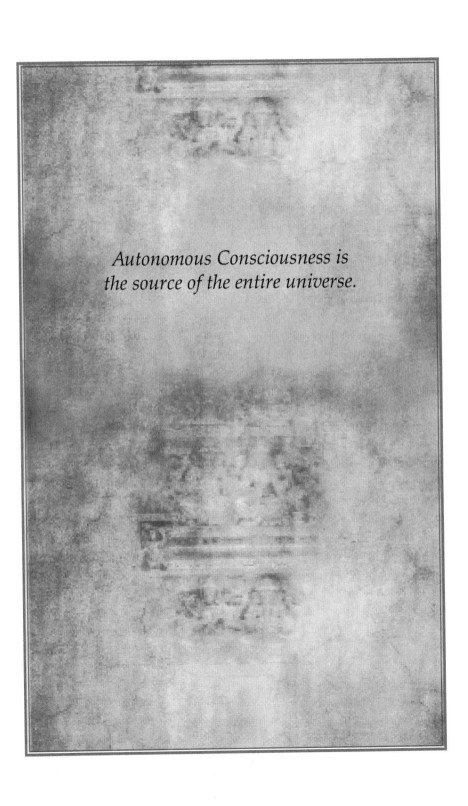

*Autonomous Consciousness is
the source of the entire universe.*

Sutra One

Tantric philosophy describes God as the unity of Shiva and Shakti. Shiva is the unbounded, eternal field of Consciousness; inherent within that Consciousness is the power to create. Consciousness is expressed and made manifest through energy, and that power is called Shakti, Kundalini, or the Goddess. There have been endless philosophical debates about the relative importance of Shiva versus Shakti, but the highest understanding is that there is only the union—what is called *Paramashiva*—or Shiva and Shakti as One. Divine reality is a singular, autonomous state of consciousness containing within it the potential to manifest everything in creation.

When we study this or any other sutra, we want to explore how it applies to our life and experience. This first sutra states that pure undifferentiated Consciousness created the universe from a state of self-sufficient freedom. We must come to understand that we are not separate from that Consciousness. Nothing is separate from It. And if we are *not* separate from this Divine Source, then our individual life is a manifestation of what we too have created, in our own freedom. If we have brought it about, what is all the fight about?

THE STRUCTURE OF CONSCIOUSNESS

There are two aspects of Consciousness that we have to consider: the power to know or perceive, and the capacity to be aware of our self-knowing. The capacity to enjoy knowing makes it an active experience. The terms for these qualities of Consciousness are *prakasha* and *vimarsa*. *Prakasha* is often described as the light that illuminates life, and *vimarsa* is the light by which the light itself sees. Watch and experience the sun rising. The subtle reality is that from the perspective of unity *we* are causing the sun to rise, and witnessing as it does. This is an example of how Consciousness creates from within Itself and is aware of that experience. How amazing that we are not separate from that Divine awareness. What happens at the end of the day? We cause the sun to go back down.

The foundation of all awareness is the capacity to be conscious and to recognize our state of consciousness. So immediately the discussion moves from the highest—from Paramashiva, Shiva-Shakti—directly to us, because, of course, there is no separation between God and ourselves. Our discussion of the tattvas later in this book will reveal that we are way down on the totem pole of creation. Individuals don't even come into existence until the twelfth tattva. Even so, we are a reflection of that highest Consciousness. One of the names for the Goddess (or Shakti) is Shodasi, which translates as "the light in the eyes of Shiva." Not *what* Shiva is seeing, but the light *by which* He sees. We are both that light and the eyes of Shiva.

The extraordinary thing about being alive is that we are conscious. This capacity for Supreme Consciousness to know Itself is the same capacity for us to know our Self. That includes knowing ourselves at whatever frequency of contraction we might find ourselves in. The first step in spiritual growth is the capacity to recognize our state, so that we can transform it. That power was given to us by our Self, our creator. What we come to understand is that even though we, as individuated expressions of God, are down the ladder of creation, it is human consciousness that has the capacity to transform itself.

We are at a pivotal point in creation. If we go further down the ladder, the levels of consciousness do not have the same capacity for transformation. A dog is a dog. A rock is a rock.

Humans, however, have the choice to remain simply human or to shift themselves into their Divinity. Inherent in the ability to be self-aware is the power to change our experience. Why would this Divine magnificence have created the universe? To have fun; to look back upon Itself and know the inherent joy of Its own existence. Even for God, being conscious isn't all it is cracked up to be if it can't be experienced. Believe it or not, *we* are how God experiences Himself!

GOD'S WILL, OUR WILL

Consciousness in Its freedom manifested the universe. It didn't have to. Nobody called or emailed saying, "Why don't you do this?" Creation is the result of God exclaiming, "Look what's coming out of My center!" The universe is what emerged—because of the desire, the will to express and experience freedom. This is worth remembering. If this Divine magnificence created the universe out of Divine will, what does that say about you and me? We are here because God willed it.

What does that say about our will? We should surrender it to God's will, which is far wiser than ours. We all know that we have a will of our own, and we all experience what happens when we exercise it. The results are not necessarily pretty. That is why I suggest that your life, in its highest, is not about "you." It is about Shiva saying, "Let's dance . . . and I need some partners." We are the partners. Stop trying to control the steps. Learn to follow.

Even when we deeply surrender it doesn't mean that some trace of our own will won't start to crop up. That is where consciousness comes in. We can become aware of our state and hopefully self-correct from that knowledge. However, every one of us has had the experience of feeling that we shouldn't be doing something and then proceeding as fast as we can to do it anyway, not listening to the deepest place in ourselves.

21

When we see our own will beginning to emerge, the common experience is that we recognize our willfulness, but, in spite of that, we continue down the same road. Why would we do that? The clue is that we get hooked by the perpetual obsession, "What's going to happen to me?" This is what has been called the mantra of stupidity, and it is the fundamental fallback position of the ego. Our ego adamantly believes it is separate from its Source, and it will fight until the end of time to defend that position. If you are not sure if a thought or action is the expression of your will instead of God's will, just get some duct tape, close the orifices of speech and action, and listen for this mantra. If you hear it, you will know that it is not God's will.

How many times do we really get quiet and listen to find out whether we're acting from our own self-interest? Not that often! We unfortunately get caught up in trying to fulfill our own needs. As we progress through the sutras, we'll see that they show us that Consciousness is everything, but that as It unfolds our individuality, our own awareness can become very limited in focus. So much of the early years of spiritual work is getting over the fact that our own stuff isn't that important. Even who we think we are is probably not correct—so we have to let go of all preconception. Then, what we think we need (based on who we think we are) has a lot less strength of conviction. If I am not who I think I am, then what-I-think-I-need based on who-I-think-I-am will likely shift.

STILLNESS PULSATES ON A FIELD OF UNITY

The only way to rise above the mantra of stupidity is to center ourselves in stillness, to recognize and rest in the Divinity that lives in our heart. In the *Pratyabhijna Hrdayam*, the highest mantra is Aham, which translates as "I Am." The awareness contained in *I Am* is total and complete and doesn't need to worry about "what's going to happen to me." The sound of the mantra is the resonance of Shiva and Shakti in unison. "A" is Shiva, "ha" is Shakti and "m" is the union of the two. It is the sound of existence, the supreme couple proclaiming their eternal freedom. (See the Appendix on page 269 for a link to a free guided Aham Mantra Meditation.)

In the Introduction I mentioned the *Spandakarikas* as one of the principal texts of Tantric philosophy. Its whole premise is that there is a primordial vibration, a Consciousness that is the foundation and source of all manifestation. Everything emerges from that impulse—but underlying even this initial vibration, present before it begins to arise, is the simple being of existence. Aham is Consciousness and energy, simply resting in Itself, and being aware of Itself. From this Source, everything manifests, including us. When we experience this, we too are complete. No longer engaged in the endless search for something to fulfill our needs, we can surrender our will to God's.

This is spiritual freedom—the experience of Unity, the direct recognition that all of life is Consciousness and energy, which are simply two aspects of the supreme reality. Only the mind wants to make a distinction between Shiva and Shakti. Just the use of language, even in scripture, creates some misunderstanding, because we're immediately talking about Shiva *and* Shakti, as if they were separate. All of these scriptures have the potential to free us . . . or confuse the hell out of us!

Although everything is Consciousness and energy, Tantric philosophy emphatically states that manifestation is real. The Vedantic tradition, on the other hand, says that there is only *Satchidananda*, "Being, Consciousness, and Bliss," and nothing else is real. There is only *maya*, or the illusion of manifest existence. The Tantric definition of maya is very different from the Vedic. Tantra defines maya as the misunderstanding that anything is separate from God, not that the universe doesn't exist. If everything is One Thing—a manifestation of God—how can it *not* be real? So there is a fundamental distinction here between the two philosophies.

RECOGNITION: FINDING FREEDOM

As we engage in the world, we have the power of will to create the life we want—and it is always on the field of God's will. Divine will is an expression of God's freedom, and it is therefore ours as well. The question is, are we experiencing our limited perspective, needs, and desires, or the unrestricted field of Divine will? Are we using our will to free ourselves from the illusion of separation? If we truly attempt to allow Divine will to express itself through us, our own willfulness is going to be exposed. We then have the choice to surrender so that our mantra becomes, "May my will be Your will. May I live in Your Grace."

If we don't surrender our will, we get bogged down in our limited field of vision. It is like going to an extraordinary buffet, finding a bowl of peanuts at the first table, and getting stuck there. We don't look further than what's right in front of our nose. We eat only the peanuts and still we haven't figured out why we have constipation and indigestion every day. That's why we must choose to get our face out of those peanuts and begin to see what else there is.

We have the same experience again and again in our lives. What's more, we repeatedly do the same things, trying to change the experience, to pull more happiness from those same peanuts. As the saying goes, "If you keep doing what you have always done, you keep getting what you have always gotten." Who will change it for you but yourself? We change by expanding our vision beyond the ego's comfort zone, beyond its fundamental belief in duality and separation. And we can do this because we have free will and the capacity to be conscious.

The bottom line of this sutra is that *your* life is your means to liberation. The same Divine Consciousness that unfolds from within Itself to create the universe is within each of us. God's inherent Consciousness and freedom exist in us every moment of our lives, and from that freedom we create our experience.

Understand how powerful that is! But the question is: What do we use that incredible power for? Normally, we use it to reinforce our separation, to solidify the ego and its limitations.

In its highest sense, liberation is freedom from yourself, from thinking your life is about you. The extraordinary thing is that this means nothing in your life has to change—although everything can—and it still has nothing to do with you. Life is not about you as an individual. Why not change your perspective? What do you have to lose, except your unhappiness? We hold on to the things that make our life unbearable and then we are angry because our life *is* unbearable.

We have a lot less control over what comes and goes in life than we want to imagine. In fact, the things that leave us or that come to us always do so to wake us up, to bring us back to freedom. Freedom has no condition attached to it. None. Day by day, we face the perfect opportunity to realize this. In any situation we encounter, we choose our experience of those conditions on a moment-by-moment basis, by focusing either on openness or on limitation. Understanding life from this perspective, we learn that everything presented to us is a gift, a chance to grow. How we react to that gift is up to us. This is what I mean when I say we choose our experience.

If we are creating an experience of bondage, it is because we are choosing to do so. We think, "I shouldn't have to experience or be doing *this*." Who said? Let God be the judge instead of you. Any judgment from a lower perspective will at best be incomplete, if not totally wrong. We have to be willing to really suspend our beliefs, let go of that which we don't know, and stop trying to understand from the place that will never understand.

From the highest viewpoint, if the Divine created us as part of the play of experiencing Him-Her-Itself, then our duty is to allow that to happen—to allow that Consciousness to fully express Itself in our lives. We have the power of that choice within us. Who are we to deny God the experience of His own joy? That would be a bit arrogant. Be grateful that you have the possibility of expressing Divine Consciousness in your life, and choose to live in freedom. If your consciousness is the means to your liberation, use it for that, and don't accept anything less.

स्वेच्छया स्वभित्तौ विश्वमुन्मीलयति

svecchayā svabhittau viśvam unmīlayati

SUTRA TWO

*Of Its own free will (that Consciousness)
unfolds the universe on the screen of Itself.*

Sutra Two

The universe manifests from an act of Divine creation, which is the supreme expression of Divine will. Even while It manifests all diversity, Its experience is of Unity. Even as It contracts to form images upon "the screen of Itself," Consciousness never loses Itself, and our lives take place on the field of that same Consciousness. Nothing separate is created. I love the phrase from the Chandoga Upanishads: "God is one without a second." God created all of this, and yet there's still not "two." The universe—all creation, all manifestation—is simply unfolded upon Consciousness, and never separate from Consciousness. It never loses contact with Itself, even as It dances.

This second sutra is a further exploration of the first, but an important element is added with the statement, "Of Its own free will." It is Divine creative will that gives rise to life and the experience of life. Will is choice. Consciousness, just floating along without a universe, chose to manifest that universe, and it did so by condensing Its infinite expanse back onto Itself.

From that contraction, a natural expansion then arises, and this dynamic pulsation unfolds from Its own center, where the vibration is so subtle that it's virtually imperceptible. And yet inherent in this subtlety is infinite power and potential. The supreme symbol of that process of manifestation is the thousand-petaled lotus, which depicts the blossoming of all the multiplicity of life from within Itself. Inside the seed of any flower is the potential for the arising into form and the subsiding back into a seed again.

In meditation we can experience that there is really no distinction between expansion and contraction. Both take place on the field of Consciousness. It's like what happens with water in its different forms. Water, which is liquid and in motion, freezes and becomes solid. If it reverts to liquid and evaporates, it becomes vapor, rises into the sky, and then returns as rain. Inherent in the water is energy—which creates a different form as it is released or absorbed—but its essential nature is always water, despite the changes on the gross level.

CONCEALING AND REVEALING

There is always the natural pulsation of life, which is expanding and contracting, arising and subsiding. This is described in Tantric texts as the Fivefold Acts of the Divine: the ongoing cycles of creation, maintenance, and dissolution, along with concealment and revelation. God has chosen to hide Himself within creation, and it is Grace that allows us to see through to the Source of all manifestation. This is what happens for us as humans. We are all born, we live for a while, and we die. That is the cycle of rebirth, over and over and over again. What changes are the acts of concealing and revealing. Which of those dominates our awareness is the key to whether we achieve liberation in a particular lifetime. In Sutra Ten we will return to this discussion of the Fivefold Acts.

When individuals contract they are, in effect, concealing their true Self. Although human contraction is essentially the same process as God hiding Himself, it happens from an already limited place within us and therefore has a different effect: suffering. When Consciousness expands and contracts, It expands, unfolds, and becomes the universe, never losing contact with Itself. It can deal with Its day-to-day activities without getting all screwed up, as we are prone to do! We all expand and contract. The question is whether we lose our center as that happens.

A person focused on spiritual growth is conscious of their state and will use that awareness to move back to center if it is lost. When we're contracting and we're not really aware of it, then we're caught in the contraction and begin to project out from there. We engage the world through the filter of our own tension, and we thereby attach our internal contraction to something, somebody, or some other. When we see that it's *our* contraction, we can extract ourselves from it, keep the energy inside, and use that energy to expand ourselves.

We are part of this ongoing, universal expansion and contraction, but problems arise as soon as we mistakenly believe we are separate from God and that our life is about us. There is a critical difference between thinking that we as individuals are in control of life and understanding that we are an expression of the unfoldment. It is only when we surrender our personal will to Divine will that our awareness rises to the Divine level—and then we know life is not about *us* but about God expressing Himself *through* us.

CHOOSING TO ALIGN WITH GOD'S WILL

The whole discussion of will boils down to the fact that we have free will to choose within the context of a higher will. And what does the higher will desire for us? That we reconnect to God and experience our freedom. That's all God wants, and He doesn't give a damn about the details. *We* make it about beating life into whatever form we believe will give us happiness. We compile a list of demands about what we must have or do, and we get very attached to these things. In reality, we can do anything, want anything, and have anything—as long as we don't *need* any of it. Mostly, we can't be attached to wanting or needing something, because it may not happen. What we want and need may not be part of the higher will that is trying to bring us freedom.

The only thing we can do is surrender and trust that there is an intelligence greater than ours at work in our lives. How could it be that the power that is capable of creating and sustaining the universe is *not* just a bit smarter than we are? Our individual will is always bucking against what God has given us. We are like a drop of water in the ocean that thinks, "I'm not part of this ocean, and I'm in control." It's silly business, yet somehow we are convinced that we are in control, so we're out there with a sledgehammer trying to mold our life. We firmly believe, "My freedom is about my (fill in the blank!), and I'm going to beat on life until it has no life in it . . . to make sure I get what I want."

We are so busy being ambitious, pushing to construct "the perfect life," that we miss what life is offering us at every moment: the experience of freedom. All of us know how often we miss that possibility because we're so busy forging our life. We think we know better than God, we don't trust God, and we don't live in surrender. The amazing thing is that the life we can imagine for ourselves is miniscule compared to the life that is available to us. The really surprising thing is that we think whatever we're clinging to will make us whole, despite the fact that time after time we are disappointed when we do actually get what we want. Not to mention that we get tied up in knots just trying to get it!

GETTING PAST OURSELVES

The arising and subsiding of limited experience is what brings us suffering. We want something; we feel must have it. We complain because we don't have it. Once we get it, we definitely don't want it—and then we suffer because we have it and can't get rid of it. This is how the mantra, "What's going to happen to me?" plays out in our lives. This is what we do over and over again, thinking, "Next time it will be different."

All the things we don't have, all the things we think we need, all the things we do have but don't want, are God showing us our life. Even the difficult and challenging moments have been given to us for the purpose of revealing our freedom. God doesn't have a return policy. Live the life you've been given from the deepest place within you, trust, and be willing to be changed. This is how you will recognize and experience Divine brilliance in all its diversity.

We've been discussing how Divine Consciousness unfolds Itself and creates the universe. It is profoundly telling that we immediately need to ask, "What about me? What about my will?" The truth of the matter is that at the level of Divine Consciousness unfolding Itself, we don't even exist yet—and so at this point there is literally no discussion of how God's will has an effect on our individual will. Yet our concern is perfect, because it clearly demonstrates our own limited consciousness and our limited capacity to perceive and recognize that there is life beyond our own existence.

Before individuality emerges there is a magnificent unfolding of Consciousness. To understand this we have to stretch beyond our own identity and what it can, or can't, perceive. In Sutra Four we will return to a fuller discussion of how Consciousness unfolds into different levels of existence, including our own. But it's natural that when we hear a description of how the universe came into being we want to fit ourselves into the picture.

It's also natural that we can't perceive of life beyond ourselves. Why? Because we have limited capacity for perception, and in order to perceive this highest level of reality we have to be willing to have that shattered. We have to be willing to let go of our viewpoint again and again—and when we truly perceive from a deeper level, that perception will shatter everything, like a rhinoceros in a china shop. This is not something that happens "eventually" in our spiritual practice. We must want that to happen right now and again and again as we grow.

This willingness to let go of ourselves is critical. John F. Kennedy made the famous statement, "Ask not what your country can do for you. Ask what you can do for your country." The Tantric version of that is, "Don't ask how life should serve you. Ask how you should serve life." Otherwise, what constantly happens is that we reduce infinite Consciousness, which is a million times bigger than we have the capacity to perceive, to something we *can* perceive, categorize, and feel comfortable about. That is why I say that your life isn't about you, except in the sense that it is your means to liberation, your means of understanding the infinite Consciousness beyond yourself.

SURRENDERING INTO FREEDOM

We have been given free will, but ultimately the highest thing we can do with our will is surrender it to God's will. Deeply surrender to God's will and let God unfold your life for you. Whatever then unfolds for you is perfect—and whatever doesn't unfold is also perfect. Permanent joy is revealed only when we live in the inner place where we understand that we are perfect whether something is taken away or added, because neither scenario changes our experience. When we tune in to that place in ourselves, we use our will to do so. We surrender the delusion that we are in control and let go of our need to change anything. We simply watch our life unfold upon itself, and there's no concern about what's happening or not happening.

Surrender is not giving up or giving in. It is choosing the will that is trying to free us. It is the offering up of our limited selves so that we can become immersed in something greater than ourselves. God becomes bigger as each individual expands God's boundaries through their liberation. This is true creative power. People are always concerned about their creative life, but what is more creative than to transform ourselves so that we can live a life of complete, permanent freedom, joy, and happiness? When that happens, who cares what the details look like?

Surrender is the highest act of our own will, and it is the only act that really accomplishes something of value. Everything else is like moving Lego blocks around. If Consciousness, of Its own free will, chose to manifest the universe, why not use your own will to manifest freedom? The creation of the universe was an act of freedom by God. The trick He played on Himself is that in the act of condensing Consciousness into form, He forgets Himself. God values the experience of freedom so much that He gave it up in order to experience the joy of remembering again!

Where did He give it up? As you and me. When we explore the tattvas we'll see that it's only at the point where individuals come into existence that the forgetting is permanent in the sense that forgetting becomes "someone's" experience. Why should we love God so much if that's what he chose for us? Because if God, in all His infinite wisdom, decided that knowing Himself through forgetting and remembering was valuable enough to put that master plan into motion, perhaps it says something about the importance of that experience in our lives. Authentic spiritual people reach to understand this.

Your life is not about you. And if it's not about you, then what you think you need, your ambition, etc., etc., simply isn't a big deal. The Tantrics help us understand that even though it's not a big deal, and *because* it's not a big deal, we can have it all. It's only when we overinflate the importance of what we have or do that we diminish our experience of the highest. It's only when we get caught in some object, some struggle, that we lose contact with ourselves. That's what limits our experience of being fully aware of the highest level of our lives, of being an expression of the pulsation of Consciousness and energy. It is really our attachment to our separation—and therefore to the importance of our individual needs and desires—that creates the conflict between our will and God's will.

RECOGNITION: UNCOVER THE EXPERIENCE OF UNITY

Seek to have the experience of unity, and don't let your mind or emotions become a barrier to uncovering that ultimate reality. Our mental and emotional constructs are not the highest expression of the gift of life. In fact, they're really not relevant except to the extent that they become excuses for not seeking the highest in ourselves. When we surrender the part of us that doesn't really know — and that definitely includes our mind, emotions, and our will — when we tune in to a deeper place inside, all our drama drops away.

We exist because of the creative joy of Divine Consciousness. That's where our urge to create comes from, and that's what our manifest life should be about. The question for each of us is, how much time do we spend in the joy of creation versus being caught in the suffering of it? One of the beautiful things about Tantric practices is that there is no rejection of the world. There is an understanding that it is an expression of the Divine in all of its joy. True *boksha*, the celebration of life, is not found just in deep meditation but in the rest of our day. That is the proving ground for how deeply we are connected to God, regardless of what is happening in the dynamics of our life.

As spiritual students, we constantly attempt to disprove spiritual reality. We think it does not apply to us. Unfortunately, most of the time, when people come to a moment of profound shift in their capacity to really open and understand, they simply withdraw. They back away from that expansion because it threatens everything they think they know about themselves. It threatens their identity as a separate individualized expression of Divinity. Okay, that is a bit scary from the perspective of the limited identity that is about to be dissolved.

I love the Sufi line, *"fana fi 'Allah'* — May I be annihilated in God."* They sing and dance it in ecstasy. Isn't that incredible? What is it that we are trying to have annihilated? Our ego. Our separateness. If we experience "me" and "God," there is still separateness. At the highest level, there is not even the experience of "me absorbed in God." There is only God, only One. What the *Pratyabhijna Hrdayam* and all authentic texts are stating is that we *are* the Supreme Being, and when we live that reality, we don't have a name anymore. Spiritual liberation is about total unity, total immersion into God Consciousness. What are we so worried about? But recognize that your perspectives, your consciousness, and your identity will get annihilated as you come to know God. I suggest to you that this is a very good thing.

तन्नाना अनुरूपग्राह्यग्राहकभेदात्

tan nānā anurūpagrāhyagrāhakabhedāt

SUTRA THREE

It (Consciousness) is diversified by multiplying into reciprocal subjects and objects.

Sutra Three

If we start from the understanding that the Supreme Subject is Divine Consciousness, then everything else is an object that is formed from that Consciousness. This includes you and me, and therefore we are the same as Divine Consciousness. The question that always arises is: Why did God decide to manifest at all? If Shiva was abiding in the bliss of His own existence, needing to do nothing, repeating "Aham," why didn't He stay that way?

Manifestation happened so that God could experience Himself as diversity, instead of as this boring Oneness thing! Out of the power of Divine will everything is created from within Himself. We hear in Tantric discussions a phrase that Bhagavan Nityananda made famous: "It is the play of Consciousness." Shiva created the universe as a playmate, just because it is fun to have one, and because that experience of play is the celebration of Shiva's own nature. But as soon as anything becomes manifest, the subject-object relationship is born, creating a reciprocity between the two.

From Aham, "I am," Shiva transitions to *Sadashiva,* "I am this." As soon as we move from *I am* to *I am anything else* we have diversity. However, at this level of consciousness there is no duality, because the diversity is not separate from its source. Duality comes into existence further down the totem pole of manifestation, with the illusion of separation. Divine Consciousness, despite all of the diversity displayed in the manifest forms of the universe, does not experience anything as different, or separate from Itself.

OUR LIMITED PERSPECTIVE

If this is the Divine perspective, why do we experience it differently? We experience separation because of the level of consciousness in which we perceive. Remember that Consciousness has two aspects, the capacity to be aware and the capacity to be aware of Itself. Shiva is aware of Himself as form. There is no separation. Shiva does not experience the three veils of duality—I am separate, I am different, I am the doer—because in truth there isn't any duality. He is the doer, but he doesn't experience it in the same way that we experience our action. His experience is only the play of Unity.

The diversity and distinction we experience arise out of our perception that subject and object are different. We think that we and our life, we and other people's lives, we and the universe, are different. Although diversity is real, the distinction of separation within that diversity is only a feature of our limited perspective. In other words, it only appears to be true within the bounds of our limited consciousness. There are many levels of consciousness, and each has a different capacity to perceive reality. At most levels the highest reality is hidden due to the density of perception and the contractions of Consciousness. When Divine Consciousness contracts, Its perception of Itself diminishes.

At our level of experience, we do find that clarity of perception sometimes arises. We get in touch with the part of ourselves that knows we are Shiva. This place of contact with our Source propels and creates our longing for realization. But we also experience the part of us that forgets who we are. Viewed from the highest perspective, nothing is different or separate from Shiva, but there is a denser capacity for awareness that happens within us as an individuated self. When we function from this denser awareness, we simply do not recognize our highest Self. The ego of individuated consciousness primarily does one thing: It perpetually reinforces itself, because that is its identity.

So we don't focus on the ego; we focus on and tune in to the part of us that knows it is Shiva.

HOW WE PERCEIVE

Just as Shiva created the universe as His own object, we, as the subject, create the objects of our life. We create: "I am a person. I am an engineer. I have negative feelings about my worth." There is "me" and "my life," a subject and an object, and our experience is that there is interplay between those things. What happens in our life has an effect on us, and, conversely, the state we live in has a lot to do with what happens in our life. That is the reciprocal adaptation, and it is a constant interplay of the flow between creation and its source.

The same reciprocal experience takes place at every level of consciousness, creating the possibility for the recognition of Unity instead of duality. The entire expansion of the cosmos is happening on the field of Its own Consciousness, and there is no separation between the expansion of Consciousness and the expansion of Its creation. We always have the choice to transform our perception because ultimately we are not separate from the ever-expanding universe. Rudi expressed this idea when he said, "You can only have as big a life as you can be open to."

Practically speaking, what happens as we go through our day is that we have this reciprocal relationship, but we forget that we created it. We firmly believe there's "me" and there's "it." In that forgetting we immediately lose sight of the perfection of our life, which is created on the screen of our consciousness. We must recognize the perfection of it, because as soon as we deem life imperfect, we immediately believe we have to change it. It is only our perception that there is something wrong with life—that it is not the way it ought to be—that makes it imperfect.

A key to our misperception lies in the veils of duality: I am separate, I am different, and I am the doer. It's easy to be caught in the veil of separation because we have a body and we identify with that aspect of our existence. That's why the death of a loved one is especially painful. We think that the person *was* the body. In Tibet, there is a ritual where the family of the deceased chops up the body and tosses it out to nourish the vultures. It is a clear statement that they view the body as "dust" and not who the person was and continues to be.

In my own life, my teacher Rudi gave me two gifts. The first was meeting him, and having my life transformed by that meeting. But the second gift was Rudi's passing—because walking into the funeral home and seeing his body freed me of any idea that he was a body. His energy was not changed by his physical death. It is only our perception that the body holds someone's awareness. In reality, the body is just a cloak over awareness. Seeing Rudi's dead body created a powerful shift in my perception.

CHANGING OUR PERCEPTION

Perception varies according to one's culture, and there is nothing in all that diversity that is right or wrong. It is real on its own level, but it is also inaccurate when viewed from a higher level of understanding. What we must recognize is that we create our own reality based on our perception. Think about your relationships with your friends, family, partner, or teacher. How we perceive what is happening between us and them creates the reality of that relationship. If we fear that someone doesn't love us, we mentally project all sorts of dramatic scenarios, which usually does nothing but complicate how we interact.

We must understand that if we want to change our reality, we must change our perception. *Sadhana*, or spiritual practice, is exactly that—the transformation of our consciousness by the Divine Force within us. But because we think that even the God within is separate from us, we fight to preserve our limited perspective. We insist on trying to change the objects or conditions in life instead of changing ourselves. That's why surrender is critical.

When we reach the penultimate of spiritual practice of recognizing our Divinity, that is the truth we come to live by, and everything else that was valid up until that point is simply no longer relevant. Don't get caught in what you don't know, or in your confusion, or in trying to understand everything. Reach inside and demand that the highest truth reveal itself, and don't be more than a little surprised when it is not what you thought it was.

These sutras, like all Tantric texts, are trying to show us our freedom—to show us that all of life is simply the pulsation of Divine Consciousness. We cannot understand this from a limited consciousness. Spiritual life is a commitment to having our own perspective, our own limited consciousness, obliterated over and over again. This may sound like a frightening prospect, but let's compare it to the simple experience that everyone has every time they feel contracted: If we find some way to open our heart, our experience dramatically changes. Given that we've all had this type of experience, why would we be afraid of the profound shift that could happen if we are able to open and know that we are not separate, but are Shiva?

RECOGNITION: THE POWER OF OUR CONSCIOUSNESS

We have the capacity to obscure the reality of God, because, amazingly enough, He gave us free will to do so. Unfortunately, we use that capacity on a day-to-day basis. Consciousness is powerful; it is the essence and source of life. We've discussed that this same power exists within us, giving us the ability to create our experience, as well as the will to create certain conditions in our life. The problem is that when we use our will to create conditions we get attached and forget ourselves in the process.

If money is our God, then life is about money. Change money to sex, power, self-rejection, etc. All of that misdirected focus comes from the power within us to create our experience in life.

Attaining our freedom is not a linear progression. We may experience the singularity of "I am" and then lose that awareness. Like the tide going in and out, we move in and out of the depth of our consciousness, but with time, we are able to move in, stay in longer, and return to our center more quickly when we lose that awareness. Through the power of our own will and attention we establish ourselves in a more permanently expanded state of consciousness, and this is how it becomes stabilized as a deeper experience.

In order to move back through the density of consciousness within ourselves, we have to reverse the process of identifying with objects within manifestation, open our awareness layer by layer, and discover the Source that underlies everything. Abhinavagupta says that in four sessions of forty minutes freedom is available to us. If our longing—our contact with that place of inspiration—was deep enough, and we could let go deeply enough within ourselves, that is all it would take to be free.

What does this say about the power of the ego to prevent freedom? The ego is as powerful as God Himself, as powerful as the Consciousness that created it. That's the beauty and the challenge of spiritual practice. That is why you have to remember that you are Shiva, moment by moment, not just during meditation, and not just when it's easy. What we typically try to do is take this process of creation, maintenance, and dissolution and transform it into being about maintaining the status quo. Even though our life is not comfortable—or at least not what we hope it might be—we fundamentally don't want anything to be changed. Isn't that interesting? The ego, our limited consciousness, likes to be comfortable in its suffering.

Although freedom is our birthright, it is up to each of us to take responsibility for realizing it. The Fivefold Acts of the Divine are always happening, and we must choose whether to focus on concealment or revelation. Even the briefest glimpse of longing is an expression of Grace. Then it's up to us how we respond to it. Our day is made up of moments; our realization is structured in the accumulation of those moments. When traditions talk about being present, living in Presence, that is what they mean. If we could surrender all diversity in one moment, then our freedom would be realized.

Even at this highest level surrender changes nothing about our life. What it absolutely changes is our experience of that life. I define Grace as the freedom-bestowing power of the Divine. What it is freeing us of is generally not what we think we need to be freed of. The operative word is "freedom." To some degree, even though we have the free will to have whatever perception we want, part of the real message is that we had better not be too attached to anything, because in our attachment, we give it reality. We give life a floor and a ceiling, and our reality exists within these dimensions. This limitation is very real, and the effect it has on our experience is profound.

If you can open your heart moment by moment, you will be free. You have to believe that. The ridiculous thing is that we don't believe it, even though we have repeatedly experienced it. We forget that, "Yesterday I was tight and then I opened and I felt really great." We think, "Today I am feeling tight and there has to be a reason—and I have to blame somebody for it!" This is what it means to be locked into our own perspective. The Grace, the revelation, is that with our eyes open, living through any experience, in all this diversity, we can penetrate through our perception and see the Source, the oneness in all that diversity. This is the power of Consciousness.

चितिसंकोचात्मा चेतनो ऽपि संकुचितविश्वमयः

citisaṃkocātmā cetano 'pi saṃkucitaviśvamayaḥ

SUTRA FOUR
AND THE TATTVAS

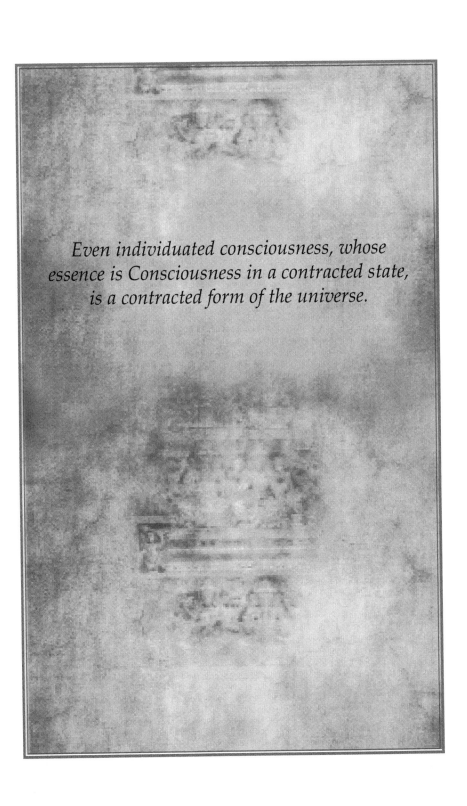

Even individuated consciousness, whose essence is Consciousness in a contracted state, is a contracted form of the universe.

Sutra Four and the Tattvas

What is the first thing this sutra says about us? It states that we are an individuated expression of the Divine whole, but in that individuating we are not different, or separate from this Source. The same underlying principle that created the universe creates our minds and bodies. To understand more fully how we come into existence, where we fall in the hierarchy of creation, and why we are not separate from universal Consciousness, it will be helpful at this point to discuss the tattvas.

Earlier we said that the tattvas are the Shaivite explanation of how manifest creation emerges from unlimited Consciousness. The tattvas describe the process by which Consciousness contracts from its universal undifferentiated state down into the lowest level of density. As we go through the tattvas we will see how, from that one single, infinite Consciousness, everything is created—and no matter what form It takes, from a supernova down to our fingernails, it is all Consciousness. However, there is a corollary to this statement, which is this: No matter what form it takes, there is a contraction of Consciousness—and it is in this contraction that the misunderstanding of separation takes place. In addition, the more Consciousness contracts, the more this misunderstanding shows itself.

This principle certainly applies to our own lives. The further we get from our Source, the more we contract. We all have had this experience. You can even watch the news and hear about some wife shooting her husband in a fight over who gets their ham sandwich! The more we misunderstand life (and fighting

Paramashiva

1. **Shiva** *Chit Shakti*
2. **Shakti** *Ananda Shakti*

3. **Sadashiva** *Iccha Shakti* 4. **Ishvara** *Jnana Shakti* 5. **Shuddha-Vidya** *Kriya Shakti*

6. **Maya** *Veil of Limitation*

Kanchukas *Limitation of*
7. **Kalaa** *Omnipotence*
8. **Vidya** *Omniscience*
9. **Raga** *Completeness*
10. **Kaala** *Eternity*
11. **Niyati** *Omnipresence*

12. **Purusha** *Individual Subject*
13. **Prakriti** *Objective Experience*
14. **Buddhi** *Intellect*
15. **Ahamkara** *Ego*
16. **Manas** *Mind*

Jnanendriyas *Powers of Perception*
17. **Shrotra** *Hearing*
18. **Tvak** *Touch*
19. **Chakshu** *Seeing*
20. **Jihva** *Tasting*
21. **Ghrana** *Smelling*

Karmendriyas *Powers of Action*
22. **Vak** *Speaking*
23. **Pani** *Grasping*
24. **Pada** *Locomotion*
25. **Payu** *Excretion*
26. **Upastha** *Procreation*

Tanmatras *Subtle Elements*
27. **Shabda** *Sound*
28. **Sparsha** *Touch*
29. **Rupa** *Form*
30. **Rasa** *Taste*
31. **Gandha** *Smell*

Mahabhutas *Gross Elements*
32. **Akasha** *Ether*
33. **Vayu** *Air*
34. **Agni** *Fire*
35. **Ap** *Water*
36. **Prthivi** *Earth*

about a ham sandwich is a pretty powerful misunderstanding), the more we act from that stance. The fact that we can kill someone because of a difference in beliefs shows how solidified in limitation people can become. Every part of Consciousness carries within it the whole of creation, yet we don't experience that in our lives. So this is where the discussion of the tattvas becomes important. (See the chart on the opposite page).

THE THIRTY-SIX TATTVAS

The tattvas help us understand how Consciousness contracts as It manifests, and how we fit in that process of contraction. Although tattva means "that-ness," the thirty-six tattvas begin by saying that supreme Consciousness and energy exist before *that-ness*. Before anything comes into being, there is Paramashiva saying "Aham," I am. There is no description of "I am." There is simply Being, in a state of autonomous freedom. Then, as the unfolding contraction takes place, the supreme subject creates an object; in other words, Consciousness "densifies." This is really what is happening when the tattvas talk about contraction. They mean that Consciousness becomes denser and denser as the entire universe unfolds.

The tattvas explain to us how, from within Consciousness, energy manifests the universe to become the creation of the one Divine subject, but from God's perspective, none of it is separate from Him. In this process of unfolding God never loses awareness of Himself, no matter what aspect of the unfolding is being experienced. The universe is the creative expression of Consciousness, and it perpetually continues to manifest from within its own center, never separate from that Source.

Central to the discussion of the tattvas is the message that although there are levels of consciousness that continually open out, the highest level should be what we seek. The wonderful thing is that we must live through, penetrate, and devour everything that manifests from Supreme Consciousness— meaning the world, duality, and our perception of everything we experience—in order to get back to the Source.

Just like the sutras of the *Pratyabhijna Hrdayam*, the tattvas start with the highest, so let's begin there.

TATTVA 1: SHIVA (THE POWER OF CONSCIOUSNESS)

The tattvas are the expression of the emission of Shiva's five powers—Consciousness, bliss, will, knowledge, and action. These are the powers of His own existence, and everything arises from them. The first tattva is called *Shiva,* and while Shiva is understood to be Pure Consciousness, it is also recognized that inherent within infinite, Pure Consciousness is an observable power. This is the source of all other powers, all other energies, and ultimately all manifestation. It is a state of dynamic stillness. This tattva is also called *chit shakti,* because it describes the energy or power of Consciousness.

TATTVA 2: SHAKTI (THE POWER OF BLISS)

The next tattva is *shakti,* which is the energy that arises from Consciousness. It is the first stirring of a Self-reflective quality that allows the Omnipresent to know Itself. And it's so wonderful to understand that the second level of awareness is *ananda shakti,* the power of bliss, the power of joy, the power of the unconditional state of Consciousness experiencing Its own existence. That joy just exploded out of Shiva. Held within His Consciousness and the power of that Consciousness is an effulgence that just can't contain itself, and its dynamic aspect begins to emerge.

As was previously mentioned, Tantric philosophy uses the terms prakasha to denote the light of Consciousness that illuminates all of life, and vimarsa to describe the capacity to see the light and to recognize, "I am that light." The light is coming from "me" and creating "me" at the same time. The highest teaching is not only that we are that light, but that we each have within us the capacity to be aware of our own state of consciousness—and because we have that power, we have the ability to change our level of consciousness.

Shakti arises *from* Shiva, but it can also be the pathway back to its Source, the gateway to a level beyond even the manifest value of energy or light. Shakti leads us to the rediscovery of prakasha, the light that illuminates life—which is beyond any form or energy.

TATTVA 3: THE POWER OF WILL

We can think of Paramashiva as being complete, simply experiencing "I am." But then an impulse arises: "What if I became something else?" From that infinitely subtle pulsation some form starts to be considered, which is described in the third tattva, *Sadashiva*, as "I am this." Sadashiva is also called *iccha shakti*—the power of Divine will. It reveals the inherent potential of supreme will to have the intention to create, although at this point manifestation has not yet happened. Shiva stirs and thinks, "I have, through my own volition, chosen to create the *idea* of creation."

Sadashiva means "always Shiva," or "I am this and it is always Me." At this level, there is only pure unmanifest Consciousness and the power of will giving strength to the impulse to create. This Consciousness recognizes that It has within Itself the capacity to choose Its experience, to choose a bigger experience than "I am." Isn't that interesting? If being "I am" is so wonderful, being "I am that" must be even greater!

But remember that contained within the will to create all of manifest existence is the will to create the play of Consciousness— the play of forgetting for the joy of remembering. The paradox is that even as forgetting takes place, every level of unfolding and every particle of creation contain within them the fullness of Consciousness. Everything in creation is already held within the field of Consciousness we call Shiva, and everything emerges because of the will inherent in that field.

As individuated expressions of Divine will, we can choose to remain locked in the limitations of our own will—and God has given us the option to do just that. Or we can surrender our will and let God's will flow through us, thereby experiencing the freedom and joy of remembrance. It is only by surrendering our will that we discover that we were never the doer in the first place. Then, any idea we may have that God's will somehow has something to do with our plan for our life, evaporates. Living in surrender to God's will is a state that is not bound by any condition or any expectation of what *should* happen.

TATTVA 4: THE POWER OF KNOWLEDGE

In the previous tattvas we saw that God has the power of will, which contains the potential to create. This tattva, *ishvara*, called *jnana shakti*, describes the power of knowledge. It is the knowledge of what God is going to do: expand his infinite freedom through manifestation. There is an inherent awareness of how the patterns and structures will create the universe, how energy will manifest into form. This is where awareness starts to exteriorize itself, moving one step away from the experience of "I am" to "I am all this." And yet, there is still no form. All of creation is still within Shiva's own Consciousness.

The interesting thing is that God is not concerned with the everyday details because His freedom is not conditioned or limited by what emits from Him. He does not need to know the details because he simply understands that it will show itself, out of its own perfection. So if it turns left or right or changes color, there's nothing that's not right. It's still part of the perfection, the expression of the infinite joy of God's own awareness.

TATTVA 5: THE POWER OF ACTION

Now that Shiva has the powers of will and knowledge, the next step is to act. *Kriya shakti* (or *shuddha-vidya*) is the power of action, the emphatic power of expression. It is only in the doing that creation becomes reality. Shiva has the power to manifest Himself in any shape, form, energy, or operation. But nothing has happened! All this is still percolating within the field of Consciousness. Within Shiva's own Consciousness the energy for creation is revving up, like a rocket ship about to launch. This is *spanda*, or vibration; an imperceptible movement that builds on itself, from within itself, and finally just explodes into action. Out of one single essence, all multiplicity emerges.

These five powers—Consciousness, bliss, will, knowledge, and action—are all functioning within infinite Consciousness, creating a self-reflective awareness of the potential for ideal form. And then it bursts forth, emitting itself as the expression of perfection. Shiva holds it and holds it and holds it, and He refines it, and then it's simply expressed as the flow of bliss manifesting as form. What we need to understand is that our spiritual work is that of penetrating back though all the form, through all the diversity, past the powers of God's emission, back to the infinite Consciousness that always is. This is how we establish ourselves in that Consciousness, so that we experience it as our own Self. By so doing, we fulfill Shiva's desire to experience Himself through us.

TATVA 6: MAYA (CONCEALING)

We now reach a critical juncture in the tattvas. All the potential for manifestation is waiting to burst forth, and now, Shiva adds a twist: He decides to conceal Himself in creation, just for the joy of remembering Himself again. *Maya shakti* is the energy of veiling, of concealing. It is how Shiva hides in plain sight. We've talked about the Fivefold Acts of the Divine: creation, maintenance, and dissolution—all of which are happening simultaneously—along with concealing and revealing. The concealing is the expansion into multiplicity. The revealing is the penetrating back through that multiplicity to recognize Oneness.

So while it is in the creative, imaginative, passionate power of Shiva to create multiplicity, it is in His power of maya, in His own power of concealing, that duality manifests. Some of the light begins to be veiled. In the first five tattvas we saw the beginning of a shift in emphasis from "I am" to "I am this." Now, in the descent of Consciousness, in the veiling of Its own self from Itself, Consciousness starts to see "I" as distinct from Itself. Although at this point in the tattvas the individual has not yet manifested, we can look down the road and see that because *we* function within maya, all three veils of duality dominate our perception. We believe that "I am separate, I am different, and I am the doer," and we experience our lives through the filter of that fundamental misunderstanding.

Keep in mind that the creation of the illusion of separation is all part of Shiva's will. Every minute particle in the universe contains the whole Consciousness, but it doesn't know it because the covering of maya has come into existence. In essence, Shiva decides to limit His own capacity for perception. Why? Because the bliss of Consciousness will be even more powerful in remembering. Its value will be even greater when Shiva can look back upon Himself, through us, and discover Himself again. This is the revealing power of Grace, which only happens because of the power of concealment.

TATTVAS 7 THROUGH 11: THE LIMITATIONS OF DIVINE POWER

Not only did Shiva create the power of maya, the illusion of separation, but he created further levels of concealment that limit our perception of Divinity. The *kanchukas* are the limitations of God's attributes of omnipotence, omniscience, completeness, eternity, and omnipresence, and they fundamentally color how we experience our lives.

In tattva 7 (*kalaa*), God's omnipotence is transformed into a limited capacity to do. We perceive our will as separate from God's and function from within our own resources, disconnected from Divine power. Omniscience gets squeezed down into a finite ability to know in tattva 8 (*vidya*)—and primarily into the inability to know the highest truth, our unity with our Source. We get trapped in the restricted human perspective and can't see past it.

Tattva 9 (*raga*) describes how God's completeness is experienced in the individual as a sense of lack and the desire for something to make us whole. Because we don't have access to God's completeness and believe we are different from Him, we start looking for something other than ourselves, something outside of ourselves in order to create a sense of fullness.

As we move into tattva 10 (*kaala*), eternity breaks apart into segments of time, resulting in the sense that life unfolds sequentially. We think something has to happen to get back to infinite unfolding, because the constant flow of Presence is not in our awareness. Another effect of kaala is that we have the idea that there's life and death, which results in tremendous turmoil in our mind and emotions.

The final kanchuka, tattva 11 (*niyati*), limits omnipresence as it creates space and causation. Unlimited, infinite everything-ness becomes space—and, because of time and the limiting of space, we then perceive life as causation. Then, we start *doing* things from a place of limited understanding and incompleteness, and the result of our self-serving action is the creation of karma.

TATTVA 12: THE INDIVIDUAL

The preceding six tattvas—which create fractals of the infinite through maya and the limiting of God's powers—are potent forces of obscuration. They are an extraordinarily refined process of One becoming two. Once this is set in motion, as all of Divine experience is limited and obscured, individuals and individual experience arise in tattva 12 (*purusha*). Shiva gets transformed from Himself to the individual—but at this point we're still not talking about any specific form that individuality might take, because as of yet, there is no body, mind, or ego. This is simply individuality, perceived as separate from its Source.

Tattva 12 can be viewed as the beginning of the fundamental misunderstanding of separation—but in terms of spiritual growth, it is also the entryway back into Unity. Individuation marks a *bindu* point, a singularity of focus, where Shiva pushed us from Oneness to duality, but Shiva's Grace can also pull us back up through that same bindu. Although we have been discussing the tattvas in terms of the descent of Consciousness into more density, it's at this juncture that we have to start considering ascending and descending at the same time.

Tattva 12 is the point where you either ascend back up, or you don't. All of the tattvas below this are expressions of how the individual's experience gets entangled in form, and by our mind, emotions, and ego. If we can transcend those levels of density on the way back up, we have the opportunity to really surrender the last barrier to living in Unity—our individuated existence as separate from God.

Remember that Shiva concealed Himself in separation, because it's all about the joy of recognition, the joy of opening our hearts and experiencing unconditional freedom. The whole purpose of individual experience is creating the potential for billions of little Shivas to remember that they are the one light of Consciousness, the light that illuminates life. We'll return to a discussion of why purusha is such a critical pivot point on the journey to freedom, after having presented the remaining tattvas.

TATTVA 13: OBJECTIVE EXPERIENCE

Almost simultaneous with the arising of the individual is tattva 13 (*prakriti*), or objective experience. Prakriti gives rise to materiality, meaning that matter and energy take on the structure of form, including the human body. It is at this moment that the process of Consciousness forgetting Itself is complete. Our experience of having forgotten our Source is the effect of purusha and prakriti coming into existence *after* the creation of the veils of duality and the limiting of God's powers. Because those forces of concealment are already in place when individuality and materiality come into being, we are born into the belief that there is a separation between subject (us) and object (everything else).

From the highest perspective, there is only Shiva—breathing and pulsating as every individuated expression of Himself. On that level there is no separation between the individual and the objects perceived by the individual. Although Consciousness has now descended from Its highest state of infinite freedom into multiplicity, from Shiva's point of view, all that exists is held within infinite freedom. From a spiritual understanding, we are made up of all the Divine powers we have discussed, carefully folded together to create the individuated expression of that whole. Individuality and the ability to perceive form are not limiting unless we choose to make them so.

It is our choice to look "up" toward our Source or "down" toward obscuration. We have, in a sense, let Shiva trick us into misconstruing His will, which is simply the expression of joy and freedom, in whatever form it takes. There is no pain or suffering inherent in individuated experience, but we turn form into suffering by trying to make things different, losing the capacity to truly experience our life as perfect, exactly as it is. Perfection is not defined in form, only in consciousness, only in unconditional awareness.

TATTVAS 14 THROUGH 16: INTELLECT, EGO, & MIND

The challenge for us as individuals is the interpretation of our experience. This is complicated by the fact that individuated consciousness, having formed a body, starts to have intellect (*buddhi*), ego (*ahamkara*), and mind (*manas*). Ego and mind, in particular, are what really trap us in our limited perspective.

Buddhi, tattva 14, is the capacity to recognize, formulate, and make decisions. It is the power of discernment, albeit a limited power of discernment. What's important to point out here, in terms of the descent of Consciousness, is that intellect arises before mind and ego. Buddhi is still part of higher Consciousness—before it is put within the grip of mind and ego, our own thought-constructs. Those thought-constructs are always about "me." They are always about distinction and trying to fix distinction. Buddhi just recognizes distinction and is fine with it. This is why decisions made based on discernment are less limited than decisions we make from our mind, and far less limited than those we make from our ego.

In the course of discussing the *Pratyabhijna Hrdayam*, we spend considerable time talking about the ego (tattva 15) because it is that part of us that can't see anything but itself, and it exists in a state of separation. *Ahamkara* is the Sanskrit term for ego, and, interestingly enough, the word starts with "Aham," *I am*. The problem is that ahamkara means "I am *me*." Shiva doesn't need to say "I am me." He just says "I am." Our ego makes a projection of ourselves that is not based in reality because it believes, "I am separate from Myself."

All struggle comes from the ego's determination to sustain its separate identity. We have a complete misunderstanding of who we are, and we project our lives based on that misunderstanding. Then, we work very hard to remain on that level of consciousness! We are, in fact, so attached to that misunderstanding that we feel we have to dig in and defend it, which only locks us more deeply in concealment.

This is where, at tattva 16, mind comes into play. Mind is a tool of the ego. We might even say it's a cancerous growth within ego. Thought-construct seeks to maintain the belief in separation, and this is why Abhinavagupta says that thoughts are the source of all bondage. The thought "I am separate" can only do one thing: bind you. The ego is the black hole of consciousness. Light moves at 186,000 miles per second and it cannot escape the density of a black hole. Consciousness moves without time and yet it cannot escape the density of the ego, which fights to defend itself and its perspective.

That is why liberation is only possible when we can free ourselves from the incessant chatter of the mind and the grip of the ego. If we understand this, we recognize that the pathway back to higher Consciousness is the consuming of the energy and the limited understanding of mind and ego. We internalize this energy into our psychic body, creating a flow within, pulling our awareness out of the level of mind and ego, and letting the psychic body refine that density of consciousness. In this way, we transmute density into fuel for our internal growth.

TATTVAS 16 THROUGH 36: THE DENSIFICATION OF CONSCIOUSNESS

These tattvas represent the further densification of Consciousness into matter. Looking at the chart, we can see that they fall into four basic categories: the powers of perception and action, and the subtle and gross elements. These tattvas are the world we live in. In terms of our spiritual growth, we seek to internalize the energy contained on these levels in order to transcend the misunderstanding that our interaction with material life is something outside ourselves.

RECOGNITION: OUR JOURNEY BACK HOME

The tattvas describe Consciousness becoming progressively denser, with less and less light of awareness shining through. The challenge is to recognize that it is impossible for our limited consciousness to understand the unlimited state. Even if we have the theoretical understanding that there is no separation, we still perceive ourselves as separate from God because our perception is inherently clouded by limited awareness. Our work is to break down all barriers to the direct realization of Unity and to surrender all that we do not understand—because the tattvas tell us we can never understand it from our minds and egos.

Just as Consciousness reveals the universe from within its center, we too reveal our universe from within our own center. This means we are responsible for our experience, and we create it from wherever we are focused in life—from our true center, or from being mired in our patterns and tensions.

The tattvas are a very sophisticated way of describing our journey back to the experience of our Self, which is really the Divine's journey back to Itself. All of this happens through the process of unfolding, through the densifying of Consciousness all the way out—and then reabsorbing the extended energy back through those levels of unconsciousness, returning to Pure Consciousness. Since we are expressions of God's creative power, this is also our journey.

Along the way—out into manifestation and back to our Source—we will have every imaginable experience. All types of experience are valid and valuable on their own level, but the question is, where do we ultimately want to be established? Do we want to continue living in the limitations of diversity or move back toward Unity? All of these levels of consciousness and categories of existence—all these levels of "that-ness"—are forever functioning simultaneously. And because this is true, we always have access to them, on whatever level we choose to connect to.

We must be careful to focus on the highest, because inherent in the journey is the process of forgetting. This is the fourth of the Five Acts of Shiva, the act of concealing. The first three acts of creation, maintenance, and dissolution just keep repeating themselves in an endless cycle. It is Shiva's choice to conceal, His choice to forget the very purpose of manifestation. But the tattvas are trying to convey to us what our experience *can* be—emphatically stating that we must focus on the fifth act, revealing, and that the state of autonomous freedom is the goal of sadhana.

It is so easy to get lost on the way back home. Anything that we allow to distract us from that journey *will* distract us. It doesn't matter whether we get sidetracked by a stupid little nonsense thing or some big emotional drama that we think is the end of life as we have known it. If we get distracted, we get off the path and we are lost for a long time. So we need help, and that comes from Grace—the revealing force that dissolves all concealment. The tattvas are the breadcrumbs that we sprinkle behind us, guiding us back to the experience of Unity, of unlimited freedom.

Understanding how everything is the expression of God's powers gives us a clue that we can have an individual will *and* be an expression of God's will at the same time. It is only by surrendering our will long enough, over and over again, that we begin to see that spiritual growth isn't so much the aligning of our will with God's as it is simply the allowing of God's will to flow through us. Of course, aligning our will with God is a good thing—much better than the use of it to serve ourselves. That's why from the very beginning of our sadhana we have to feel our heart, open, surrender, and live in service to others.

On the return journey into freedom, once we have broken through living in the grip of the ego, we will encounter a moment in which we have to decide whether we are going to be an expression of God's will and Grace or whether we're going to hold on to our own will. That critical point is tattva 12, where the individual stands at a doorway that can lead back through the powers of concealment, back through maya, into Unity.

Even though the power of duality created the individual, contained within the limited experience of this individuated consciousness is the innate knowing that there is no separation. As we begin to ascend back through the tattvas, all the hubble, bubble, and struggle that we make in our lives is not worth a damn if we don't get back to this point—to the recognition that we are an individuated expression of the Divine, because it is at this moment that we can begin to truly free ourselves.

चितिरेव चेतनपदादवरूढा
चेत्यसंकोचिनी चित्तम्

citir eva cetanapadād avarūḍhā
cetyasaṃkocinī cittam

SUTRA FIVE

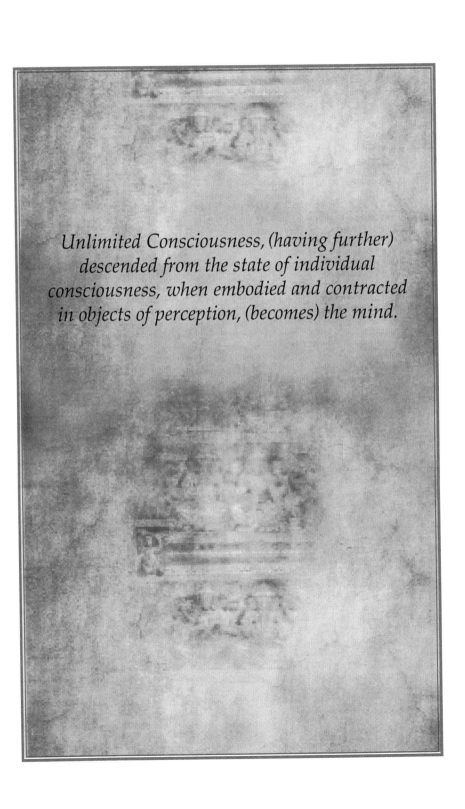

*Unlimited Consciousness, (having further)
descended from the state of individual
consciousness, when embodied and contracted
in objects of perception, (becomes) the mind.*

Sutra Five

As Divine awareness contracts and descends from its unlimited state, it gets denser and it becomes the mind. This is not inherently bad, but it becomes a problem in our lives because the mind has a limited capacity for perception. Although it can't understand its own source, the mind is the center of activity for the individual. Our thoughts and feelings arise from the mind's limited understanding, which is the result of its limited perspective. These thoughts, feelings, and the perspective of the mind are the very activity that obscures its own Divinity. Even though it is part of the whole Divine Consciousness, inherent in its experience is limitation and the obscuration of true reality.

The mind is like a spider in a giant cobweb. The spider perceives the web to be the entire universe; it doesn't know that it is located in a garden, which is on an island, in the middle of an ocean, on a planet that is one of countless others in a galaxy. The spider knows only its own small world, and that is its capacity for consciousness. Despite its inflated opinion of itself, the mind too has a limited capacity: It is a limited organ of perception.

The mind defines. It perceives a separation between itself as the subject and what it calls "not me," or the object. If there is no separation, there is no need to define. "I am" is a statement of undifferentiated Oneness, but "I am x, y, or z" is clearly an expression of the perception and the belief that there are two. I am separate from *it*, and therefore *I* am *this* and *it* is *that*. God always knows He is simply One, but inherent in the reciprocal relationship between subject and object is the potential emergence of duality, as Divine awareness descends into the limitation of mind. What does this tell us about our own experience of duality? It happens in the perception of the mind. The experience itself is what creates dualistic consciousness and it limits our capacity to experience Unity.

THE MIND AS THE FILTER OF OUR EXPERIENCE

This mind is an inherent part of the emergence of individuality, and ingrained in the mind is the constriction of perceiving. It is this limited awareness that has the need to perceive separation and to define its experience of the world. Our own experience of being happy or unhappy is a fluctuation of the mind. That makes our mind at one moment our friend and at another moment our enemy. The mind is always the instrument of duality. It defines our experience of "I am separate, I am different, and I am doing," and it does this through projection, perception, and objectification. When we think, "I am different from you," our mind is making "you" an object.

Even the people we love are seen as objects because they are separate and different from us. When we think we are different from somebody, the next step is to think we are better than them, followed by the desire to control the other person, and then the relationship breaks down. The point of relationships is freedom, not ownership. Relationships will fail if they are based on our needs. The only true need we have is to free ourselves from our misunderstandings, and it's only when we approach the other person from that perspective that both parties can grow.

Duality has one purpose—to divide one into two. Any experience of duality is limiting the experience of Unity. From the platform of duality we may still glimpse Unity, but there is always a subtle veil between the experience of Unity and duality. Tantric philosophy describes an intermediate stage of perception as "Unity in diversity," which distinguishes it from just the perception of diversity. The definition of this level of awareness is that we begin to recognize that all diversity is simply happening on a field of Unity. There is a sense of Oneness, and there is a sense of two. This is a transitional stage, part of the progression we move through as we open our awareness to higher Consciousness.

It's rare that a person progresses from experiencing duality to experiencing Oneness without passing through this middle phase—which we could call a gradation of experience—as we begin to perceive the Source that underlies and permeates everything. The mind, in a descended form of the expanded state, is where our understanding begins to pivot one way or the other: from being stuck in duality to opening to Unity.

As we discussed in the previous chapter, it is not until tattva 12 that the individual manifests. Soon after comes tattva 14, buddhi, or intellect, followed by ego and mind. You can't really separate these because buddhi also means awareness and the mind is a contracted form of Divine awareness. These particular tattvas, numbers 12 through 16, are linked together as aspects of the emergence of the individual. It is so beautiful the way the tattvas present this, because individuality is the ground upon which all other experience takes place. In Tantric discussion, the mind is really defined as thought-construct, not intelligence. Intellect shows up, and then it diversifies into intelligence, the capacity to think, and the capacity to attach our awareness to something.

LETTING GO OF THOUGHT-CONSTRUCTS

Not being caught in the mind does not mean spacing out, and it has nothing to do with the functioning of the intellect. Using our brain to think and interact with the world is very different from thought-constructs, which are the structures we continually build to define reality through our own perspective. We can drive a car sixty miles an hour while remaining in our center. Paying attention to the road is not a problem. We can distinguish that kind of practical thinking from spinning out scenarios like, "Wouldn't it be wonderful if I had a new car? . . . Wouldn't my friends be impressed? . . . Maybe my boss will take me more seriously if I show up in an expensive new car." Thought-constructs generate an endless stream of such nonsense, and we tend to get stuck in them. That is where the problem lies. There is a state called *nirvikalpa samadhi,* in which our awareness is not affected by thoughts.

Everything happens on the field of Consciousness, so in that sense even our mental noise is part of life. The question is: Where is your focus? Where is your center? When we are established in the stillness of our true center, we can immediately recognize when a thought-construct begins to take a stronger form— catching our awareness and taking on a life of its own. If we can notice this point, we can avoid letting our thoughts and emotions grip us and pull us out of ourselves.

We defined "spanda" as the pulsation of Consciousness in stillness. Thoughts are one type of energy that arises from the stillpoint in our own center, and if we can tune in to that stillness, we develop the capacity to see thought-constructs as they are just beginning to emerge. We see the initial rising of that impulse and are able to let go of it before it solidifies into form—and before we get caught up in that form and the endless stream of thoughts that then flow out from it. This is rather like watching the waves rise up from the ocean. One follows another, but there is no reason to think one wave is more important than another. We can cease to give validity to what is just the natural arising from the ocean of Consciousness, from the pulsation of spanda. There is no rejection of anything, but there is the understanding that thoughts are real only within their own context.

In order to reach that state of nirvikalpa samadhi, the first thing we must do is stop reacting to the fluctuations of the mind.

Stop believing the mind. Stop believing that you have to follow a thought to its conclusion and then act on it. We can watch the impulse of thought-construct as it arises and let it go of it at that point. Usually we don't let go. We allow a thought to take form, and then we complain, "Oh, look at the mess my thoughts created." Then the only recourse is to untangle ourselves from that knot.

INTERNALIZING OUR ENERGY

The good news is that we can untangle ourselves by taking our attention back out of whatever has solidified. The trick is to let go of the thing that you are holding on to, whatever it is that hooked your mind. Let go and then start to pull the energy back into your center—but don't be surprised if the thought behaves like a fish on a line. It might get away from you in its fight to perpetuate itself, and you could get overshadowed by the content again. At that point you can only do what expert fishermen do: alternate between reeling in and then extending the line to let the fish run, until eventually there is no tension left in the line and you finally can pull it all the way in.

We have to be aware that it is never a matter of fighting with anything but of cultivating a sensitivity to what's happening and then developing the conscious capacity to pull energy out the dynamic. The problem is that mind creates its own reality, and we become attached to that reality. Furthermore, we believe we have to control life to keep reality the way we think it ought to be. But remember that all this drama is happening on a field of undifferentiated awareness. That's why when the mind hooks us, when it creates a situation we feel invested in, we have to bring our awareness back to our center and detach from the scene the mind created.

One of the critical, pivotal points in our sadhana is cultivating the ability to separate from the reality the mind creates. In order to be free from our own thought-constructs, the key is to bring ourselves back into the expanded state from which the mind descended. We reorient our awareness toward higher Consciousness and away from the differentiation created by the mind. We do this by repeatedly engaging and immersing ourselves in our Source, both during meditation and as we move through our day.

In my practice we use a technique called the "double-breath" (described in the Appendix) to internalize energy and move it through our psychic mechanism—the chakras that make up the energetic body. The double-breath is the means by which we take the energy out of a thought, pull it back into our awareness, and then use that energy to move deeper into ourselves. The extraordinary power of the double-breath is its capacity to extract us from whatever we have extended ourselves into that has caused us to lose our center. At the same time, we take the energy of whatever trapped us and refine it into internal rocket fuel to propel us into a state of greater openness.

I used to love walking in New York with my teacher Rudi. His center was in his navel and that chakra functioned like a giant street-cleaning truck, vacuuming in energy as he moved down the street. Rudi understood that everything was energy, and that he could internalize it all. He actually sought out experiences that other people might avoid, just to pull in the energy from the density of life. It was amazing to watch him get bigger and bigger as he sucked in anything in his path. It was his expanded state of openness and flow that created that vortex.

THE UNWAVERING FOCUS ON YOUR SOURCE

Our problems are just part of what unfolds from the field of infinite Consciousness. It is the reversal of this process, the refolding of energy back into the infinite, that solves any problem. In fact, it is Shiva who solves it, not us. Our job is to recognize that He is the only doer in this entire scenario. If we think we are separate and different from Consciousness, then we think we are the doer and we lose the experience of Unity. Without that misconception, everything is simply perceived as an unfolding within the field of Unity, and there are no problems. We actually thrive and grow by absorbing the energy from any situation.

The discussion of the tattvas helped us understand that it is everything that happens after the inception of individuality that creates our own individual experience. This includes everything in our mind and emotions—our feelings of self-rejection or self-worth, our need for a partner, our insecurity about money, and so on. All of that unfolds from our individuation. We therefore should think very carefully about how much time and energy we spend struggling to resolve these issues, instead of focusing on the source of all misunderstanding, namely, our emergence as a separate entity.

The enormous struggle to change and control life becomes meaningless for people whose primary focus is liberation. That type of activity and drama is a profound distraction from truly coming to the place of freeing ourselves from separation. That is why many traditions reject the world and advocate living in a monastery or cave in order to avoid distractions. But wherever you go, there you are. In reality, the world is not a distraction; it's our perception of it and our projection into it that becomes a problem. All struggle emerges from the birth of separation and from our subsequent attachment to our identity. Simply stated, all struggle stems from the ego. All of it.

At the same time, in terms of our progression back into a higher Consciousness, life *is* full of meaning. We have to go through the world to be free of it. It is in penetrating through duality, in all of its diverse aspects, that we find Unity. This is the fundamental canon on which all Tantric practices are built. We live and experience in the world. Not only that, but we can do our spiritual practices in the midst of any amount of engagement in the world. We do not need to find a mythical "simple life" in order to do that. When we think we need to change the conditions of our life in order to do spiritual work, that's just a reflection of confusion, created by the mind. The only issue is whether we get caught in diversity and can't find the underlying unity of life.

Although I lived in an ashram for thirty years, that experience was not one of living apart from society or avoiding the ordinary responsibilities of life. Quite the contrary. I worked very hard at several jobs, including some ashram-owned businesses, and the latter sometimes required that I commit myself eighteen hours a day, seven days a week. None of that stopped me from doing my inner work.

Soon after I joined the ashram, I needed to find a job quickly, so I took the first one I could find. It was in a meat-packing plant, in the department that made hamburger patties, hot dogs, and bacon. I worked on what I called the "bacon-makin' machine," which was rather dangerous to operate. I threw the side of an animal into the machine and then slammed it shut, and this compressed the meat and formed it into a square slab. Then you pulled down levers that activated some blades that sliced the bacon. Down it went onto a conveyer belt, where six chain-smoking, gossiping women, with bouffant hairdos cemented in place with horrible-smelling spray, put the bacon into packages.

This was the environment I worked in, and it shattered all my preconceptions of what an "ideal" situation for spiritual practice should be. First of all I was a vegetarian, so I had to let go of some boundaries in order to work in a plant that processed meat. Then, I had to listen to these women carp all day, every day—and even interact with them from time to time. Finally, I had to be very careful not to add my fingers to the pile of meat that went into the machine. I had to pay close attention to what I was doing. But amidst all the noise from the machine and from the women . . . guess what? I did my spiritual work. I could not imagine telling Rudi that I couldn't take the job or that

I couldn't do my inner work while there. I had to engage the world completely, and yet from my center.

Despite the pressures of this and other jobs I held, including one as CEO of a multimillion-dollar consulting and publishing business, there was never a moment in which I said that my life was too complicated. A statement like that is just the creation of the mind. All of the responsibility and all of the work was, in fact, the fuel that freed me from my mind. When we understand that all of life is simply energy—that it is the fuel we need to reenergize our psychic mechanism—we have no need to reject the world or desire that it be simpler.

RECOGNITION: STAYING CENTERED IN OUR HEART

Perception of distinction is created by the mind, which is a contracted form of unlimited Consciousness. But if we are aware of this critical moment, in which our mind has created and identified with densification, we can create a turning point in our awareness. We can rest in our hearts instead of projecting into objects—reversing the process of awareness getting stuck in duality—and begin moving back toward an experience of Unity.

Your heart is your portal into higher Consciousness. That's why Rudi so directly said, "Take your mind and stick it in your heart." As we discussed, when that initial impulse of mind begins to arise, if we simply give it no form, we can then allow the energy of the impulse to be reabsorbed back into the heart. This is how we avoid the unfolding of thought that normally happens from the mind. Every moment of every day is an expression of the repetition of that cycle of arising and subsiding, and therefore, every moment provides an opportunity to reabsorb the density of mind back into Consciousness.

The farther we let a fish run out on the line, the more reeling is required to pull it back. It is the ability to be aware of where our consciousness is focused that determines our experience of openness versus contraction. It is in that pivotal moment, when our energy and consciousness want to descend into a limited understanding, that we can say, "I don't need to go there." This is our conscious choice. We must have the disciplined inner practice to exercise that choice, and the muscles of discipline develop moment by moment. Through repeatedly re-centering ourselves in stillness, we create the inner strength to stop ourselves from being swept away by our own thoughts.

In spite of what we want to believe, we do not have to sink into deeper levels of unconsciousness, or limited capacity, in order to free ourselves. We do not need to dwell on our limitations or analyze and understand the source of our problems. That is not how we transcend our boundaries. We are up to our necks in quicksand. Give up the idea that you have to sink into it, feel it, and experience every nuance of it. It is not true. As Rumi said, "You've been stony for too many years. Try something different." We have all been there and done that. We have sunk far enough down into those limited experiences of our lives. I am continually amazed at how much we fight to hold on to our limitations rather than work to move into a completely different level of experience.

It is by opening our heart that we stop our consciousness from condensing. And it is by opening our heart that we reverse the process when our consciousness *has* contracted. It is in the moment when our awareness descends into our mind that we have to recognize that it has done so, and ask, "Where is my GPS? Where was it that I really wanted to go?" With GPS devices you can set the system to beep whenever you start to get off course. We should have that same alert system in our own heart so that any time we start to contract we can reverse our direction.

It is imperative that we recognize this spanda moment—the opportunity to remain centered in our expanded state instead of allowing our energy to become mired in limitation. Instead of allowing the mind to create form from that limitation, trapping us in an endless cycle of thought-constructs, we can recognize that the unfolding is only a manifestation of Oneness. When we experience the unfolding as the natural expression of the diversity within Unity, there is no distraction, no limiting of our awareness. We use our mind as the doorway into expansion instead of contraction.

तन्मयो मायाप्रमाता

tanmayo māyāpramātā

SUTRA SIX

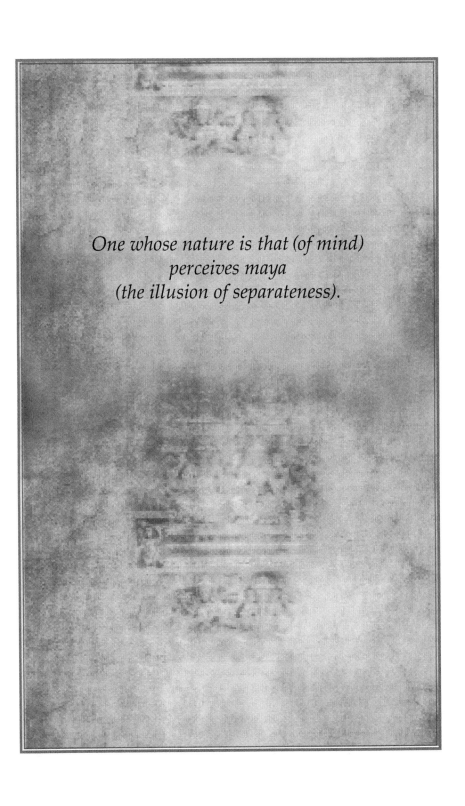

One whose nature is that (of mind)
perceives maya
(the illusion of separateness).

Sutra Six

After infinite Consciousness condenses to the level of mind, the individual functions within that limitation and we experience maya, the illusion of separation. A very interesting translation of maya is, "that which ensnares." When the expanded state of Consciousness is covered up, our life is like being in a deprivation chamber. We can't see anything, and therefore we start to imagine a lot. The mind begins to create, but because the mind is a consciousness that has descended from an expanded state, it has a limited capacity for awareness, beyond and outside of itself.

Consciousness is everything, and the tattvas are the explanation of how the unlimited state condenses into manifestation. As each level of condensation happens, the nature of that level carries through into subsequent ones. Illusion is set in motion well before the individual experience arises, and yet it has a profound effect on our experience. Shiva declares, "If I am going to ensnare Myself, then I am going to make sure that this bondage also shows up once the individual becomes the experiencer." Because Shiva decided to ensnare Himself for the joy of remembering, maya can be perceived as a gift rather than as a curse. Shiva wanted to give us the experience of having forgotten, so that we too can have the joy of remembering. How nice of Him!

This gift is another way of describing Grace. The Divine will within us has given us both maya and the capacity to be free, but our will alone is not sufficient to give us the capacity or the strength to free ourselves. Grace is what truly helps us penetrate through our density and experience the highest within ourselves. Rudi said, "Nothing has value unless you are consciously aware of it." Freeing ourselves from the ensnaring illusion of maya has value because we experience it. It has no value to those people who don't free themselves. Without freedom, life revolves like a merry-go-round, and we get dizzier and dizzier as we ride.

SEEING THE WORLD CLEARLY

This is not to say that the world is unreal. As we've discussed, some philosophies describe maya in those terms, describing all manifest reality as illusion. The Tantric understanding is that the world is real; it is just the manifest expression of God. What is unreal is the misunderstanding that anything is separate from God, and this is the illusion this sutra speaks of. When we are caught in maya, we see the world not for what it is, but what we project it to be—a very profound and subtle distinction—and our experience is based on that projection.

Maya is an expression of our limited understanding, and it has an extraordinary effect on our experience. We create our own reality. It cannot accurately be called a false reality, but it is certainly a misunderstood reality. Then, we experience what we created and work to reinforce our limited perspective, which is all we know. So maya is true because it is our experience, but it is not the ultimate truth. This is a critical distinction, because we get very attached to *our* truth and defend it with every breath. We attack in order to win and to prove that we are right. True *sadhakas* (spiritual practitioners) must seek to have all they know disproved.

When we reach deep inside ourselves, an inner consciousness awakens and begins to push away our misunderstanding. There may be struggle, pain, and resistance, but all of that is our reaction against a higher understanding that is arising in us. We may also feel as though life is shifting in a way that leaves us feeling discombobulated, but this is a good thing. It simply shows that life is changing and we are growing. We make change difficult because we immediately start trying to put ourselves back into a box instead of saying, "Hallelujah."

CONDITIONALITY AND UNCONDITIONALITY

As maya covers our lives like a fog, our fundamental experience is that we perceive life as bound by condition. This is the illusion we function in. Whether the conditions are external or internal, we are immersed in the illusion that we are *not* unconditional Divine Consciousness, and we therefore begin to lose our ability to choose freedom. We remain bound by our individual experience, and find that conditions *do* have an effect on our state. As we move through life in this way our bondage creates more contraction, which limits us even further.

The natural consequence of this experience of limitation is that we come to believe that we need something in life to change in order to feel fulfilled. We attach ourselves to some desire, thinking it will solve the emptiness we feel. Remember that in the descent of Consciousness described in the tattvas, Divine will becomes limited, eventually emerging as individual will. When we experience that we are separate, we think we need something more in order to be whole again, and we then use our will to try to create a condition that will fulfill us. We seek something new in life—perhaps a new partner or a different job. As our desires begin to dictate life, we begin to project, reach, and create a still more diverse illusion. And, as illusion begets further illusion, after a while we forget what we were searching for in the first place. This is how we lose our center.

Even when we do have a desire fulfilled, we usually experience only fleeting happiness. Over time, whatever has come into our life doesn't satisfy us anymore. Then, we think something else will do the trick and we're back on the same merry-go-round, with one desire leading to another. From the moment individual consciousness arises, we begin to project and create more diversity, more limited consciousness—rather than turn our awareness inward and go the other way. If we can move back toward a state of consciousness in which the illusion doesn't exist, then limited desire and misunderstanding do not arise.

The moment we appear as an individual we have free will, which includes the choice to be free. That freedom comes from recognizing the highest within us. It has nothing to do with our life, our careers, or our relationships. Those details are important on one level, but they are only the by-product of Consciousness. If we believe we are separate, then illusion perpetuates itself. But we can choose something different. We can be fully engaged in life and not get caught in the cycles of projecting desire.

My teacher Rudi said he "had a million things running at the same time." He had a prosperous importing business, taught meditation classes, traveled around the world, and developed an ashram system and retreat center. The amazing thing about him was that he was always tuned in on all levels. He dealt with the details of his business and ashrams while remaining fully connected to the Source of all activity. Rudi's life demonstrated that spirituality does not mean falling into inactivity, thinking that God wants us to live in silence. God wants us to be free— and there are no conditions attached to living in that state, no requirement of what an ideal life should look like on the surface.

CHANGE REQUIRES FLEXIBILILTY

People resist change because the ego wants life to appear a particular way and we cling to what we know. We want to remain in this comfort zone, even if it isn't always that comfortable!

My experience as a teacher is that people often leave a spiritual practice when they come up against something that needs to be profoundly changed within them. Instead of surrendering their tensions and making that change, students begin projecting that there is something wrong with the teacher or the practice. I have watched this for forty years.

You have to be conscious and aware. This is why Rudi spoke about "work" and "tests." We work and work, and then we are tested to see if the deepening awareness we made contact with is really our own. Higher awareness is only ours if we can express and exhibit it in the face of any condition.

Everything is Divine. It is a question of whether we recognize it. Rudi told a wonderful story about a train ride he took in India with one of his first teachers, the Shankaracharya of Puri. They were to spend the night in a section of the train that had many berths closely packed together, separated only by curtains. Rudi put the Shankaracharya in one of those beds and he slept some distance away. In the middle of the night Rudi heard a truly horrible sound, rather like a cow dying, which he soon realized was someone snoring. Rudi couldn't sleep. He got up, went searching for the offending party, and as he zeroed in on the berth and opened the curtain, he realized it was the Shankaracharya bellowing away—and Rudi instantly switched gears and thought, "What a sweet sound."

We need to develop the flexibility to disengage from any ruts we have dug for ourselves. Tibetan traditions talk about the wheel of *samsara*, the repetition of misunderstanding that we are trapped in, lifetime after lifetime. When we pull back from the particulars of this life, we can see that we've been perpetuating the same patterns since time immemorial. As we've discussed, from the inception of individuated life, the cycles of desire and misunderstanding arise, causing us to run like blindfolded hamsters on a wheel.

Samsara happens through the power of Consciousness to create illusion and misunderstanding and is perpetuated by the nature of our limited mind. Underneath this obscuration is the power to recognize the illusion, and to get off the wheel. We can reverse the process and turn the manifest awareness back into Itself. The practice of spanda is one of recognizing the point where awareness turns into thought—and from there we can stop feeding that energy and thereby stop feeding the arising of form and separation.

CHANGE ALSO REQUIRES DISCIPLINE

There is a dual process happening in us. One part of us is unfolding and expressing higher Consciousness. We know, "There has to be more to life than this." Another part reflects the mind's desire to perpetuate itself, and it digs in to maintain the status quo. It takes time to grow spiritually because the mind, the instrument of the ego, has as much power as Divine Consciousness to create our experience. We have a lot of obstacles and resistance to burn through. It takes a while to dissolve all these inner barriers, and every time we think we have gotten past a few levels we will forget for a second—and our resistance rises up and gets bigger again. That's part of the journey, and it's why discipline is required.

In time, we are able to recognize some runaway energy while we are still centered in our heart. From there, we can witness the mind starting to spin out and stop it before things get out of control. So watch your emotions, watch your thoughts, because otherwise they will build in intensity and run you over. Be aware of what's happening, but don't give it life or validity. This sutra emphatically tells us that everything that emerges from the mind is inherently mired in illusion and misunderstanding. Not some of it, not just the parts we're willing to surrender—every last bit of it.

Again, "illusion" does not mean that something is not real. It means that when we perceive something as "not God," we are simply expressing our misunderstanding that *anything* could be separate from God. Illusion here means "concealing" the true nature of existence. We, unfortunately, want to take the profound gift of life and make it about little mundane details. Then, we get so caught in those things that we completely lose ourselves and forget that the purpose of our life is to experience Divinity.

The details of life include our mental and emotional constructs, including self-rejection, self-doubt, and all the other psychological limitations we feel. They are real on their own level, and yet none of them have to be changed in order for us to make contact with our Self. Altering our psychology will not affect whether or not we're connected to our Source. We don't have to understand every aspect of how and why we feel as we do, or what caused us to misunderstand the nature of life; we just have to get in contact with Spirit. Otherwise, we can get stuck in the quagmire of our personal issues.

If we can deeply penetrate into our Self, our psychological problems will disappear, because they no longer have anything to grip on to. They cease to bind us. Spiritual life is about penetrating through the surface level that is creating a problem, and transcending to a deeper place within us. Healing comes through surrender. Practically speaking, that means we stay centered, don't allow the mind to develop runaway thought-constructs, and tune in to the part of us where nothing ever needs to be healed. Source comes through and we change our resonance. We didn't fix anything. We didn't change anything. We just tuned in to the purity that heals everything.

RECOGNITION: THE HEART DISSOLVES SEPARATION

The critical point to understand is that our perception of being ensnared happens through our mind, even though its source is

Divine Consciousness. All illusion, all limited perspective, and all misrecognition of the true nature of reality happen in our mind. This is a powerful statement—and all great saints have expressed the same idea.

The *Pratyabhijna Hrdayam* tells us that liberation happens through recognition of the Self, and this sutra emphasizes that the mind can either be a barrier to that recognition, or the point from which we can begin to turn back to our Source. Since all misunderstanding comes from the mind, it's important that we don't believe our mind but tune in to a deeper reality. This transition usually unfolds over time, although at some point, once we have opened our hearts long enough and deep enough, we are able to stop fighting with ourselves. Our work is to keep opening until that fundamental level of struggle is gone.

The real shift begins when we become aware of the mind and its activity, versus being a prisoner within it. A key element in this transition is a change in focus regarding what we are trying to solve. Instead of trying to change our psychology or figuring out why we feel as we do, it would be wiser to discover why we don't love and experience God. All of our psychological issues are really a surface expression of this same underlying problem. We just don't know it until we dig beneath the superficial layers of drama that we constantly engage in. Spiritual life is like drilling for oil; in the process we might hit levels of sediment along the way, but we should be careful not to get caught up there.

Energy and Grace will open your heart and dissolve all your problems. When we tune in to a deeper consciousness, it changes everything. But if we are so busy trying to change everything, we will not tune in to a deeper consciousness. There are many levels of maya, but the deepest level is the illusion that we are separate from the God who is always present within us. Until we *are* the voice repeating, "I am," there will always be levels of understanding and misunderstanding. Interestingly enough, one of the greatest obstacles to our spiritual growth *is* our spiritual growth. We have to be careful not to get too attached to any level of understanding. If, on the way, we get stuck thinking we've reached a fixed state of enlightenment, we'll still be stuck.

You'll never be able to figure out the paradox of separation or experience Unity from your mind. There is a great story about Saint Augustine. He was walking on the beach pondering the mystery of the Holy Trinity, trying to understand its meaning. He came upon a little boy digging a hole in the sand. The boy repeatedly ran into the ocean, filled up a small bucket, and poured it in the hole. Saint Augustine finally asked the boy what he was doing, and he replied, "I'm going to pour the entire ocean into this hole." Saint Augustine sighed and said, "I am sorry to tell you this, but you will never be able to put the ocean in this hole." The little boy looked at him with a twinkle in his eye and said, "I will put the ocean in this hole before you figure out the Trinity in your mind!"

Perhaps we ought to suspend our defense of our mind and really try something different. Let go and stop the struggle to figure everything out. Lay down the need to comprehend from your own limited perspective and allow true understanding to reveal itself. Open your heart, again and again. Take all of the mental perspective and put it into the inner flow and use it as fuel to create a more permanent place of openness within yourself. By doing this we expand our awareness back into higher Consciousness. The mind and ego get absorbed back into their Source, where there is no separation. That is how liberation takes place.

स चैको द्विरूपस्त्रिमयश्चतुरात्मा
सप्तपञ्चकस्वभावः

sa caiko dvirūpas trimayaś caturātmā
saptapañcakasvabhāvaḥ

SUTRA SEVEN

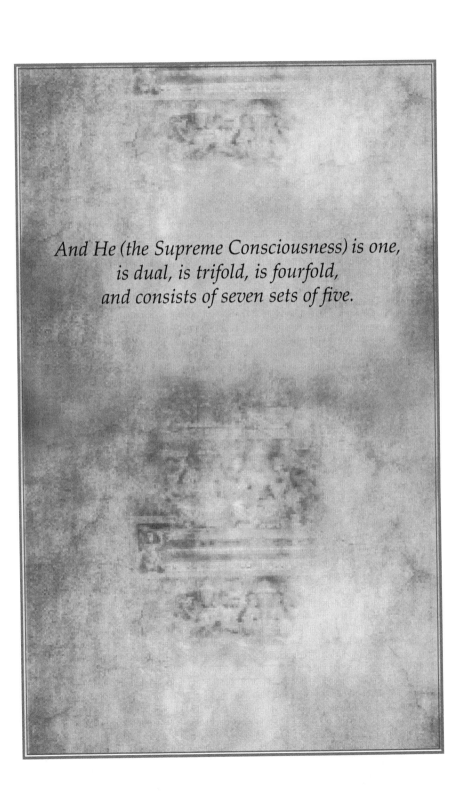

And He (the Supreme Consciousness) is one,
is dual, is trifold, is fourfold,
and consists of seven sets of five.

Sutra Seven

We have seen that autonomous Consciousness is the indivisible, all-pervasive Self. God is pure existence—the supreme reality proclaiming, "I am." Everything that emerges from this state is an expression of God's Oneness, and, as creation manifests, there are innumerable levels of complexity that come into existence. However, all of it rests on a singular field of Unity.

When one becomes two—when there is a subject and an object—we can say that God is dual. God Himself only experiences One, but there is the perception of duality. Why did one become two? We've seen that God did this simply for the joy of experiencing Himself. If that Divine Consciousness decided that It would change Itself to expand Its own experience of joy, perhaps there is a message for us. Perhaps we can open and change so that we can have what God's having!

In the Bhagavad Gita, Krishna says, "The one Self of its own accord has become Me, as an individual, and My world with all the diversity and distinction of that day to day life experience." Our day-to-day life experience is how the Divine chose to experience Itself, how It chose to experience Its own Divinity. God did that by creating all this diversity, but not as something separate from Himself.

We ought to appreciate and engage our daily life as a living expression of the Divine, instead of experiencing it as something different—like tension, stress, or desire. If we perceive only through the prism of those emotions or thoughts, then we get caught in confusion and experience something other than the infinite joy of creation. We have the opportunity to understand Unity instead of duality—and we do this in the context of the life we have been given, not by retreating from life or in some ideal life that we imagine we have to create.

The Supreme, as It contracts, forms three limited states of consciousness, which are: I am separate, I am different, and I am the doer. After One became two, two became three, enmeshed in the veils of duality. We don't see ourselves as the Oneness that became two; we see ourselves as separate from Unity. We live in this field of duality, but we don't experience its source in our lives because we are bound by the perception of separation. We don't connect the dots and see that there is a One that became two; instead, we are just entangled in the trifold veils.

THE FOURFOLD STRUCTURE OF THE INDIVIDUAL

The fourfold aspect of God becomes the structure of the individual. Tantric texts describe the fourfold structure of the individual as the causal body, the pranic body, the subtle body, and the physical body. The causal body is the consciousness that travels between lifetimes. It is what appears as an individuated form, even before we take a physical body, and remains after we take our last breath. It is the breath inside the breath. But everything is held within Consciousness, so as the causal body moves from one life to the next, our karma moves with it.

The pranic body consists of energy. It is Kundalini, the vital force that emerges out of Consciousness to give life to the individual and to create all manifest form. The causal body is Consciousness and the pranic body is energy, so here is another display of the relationship between Shiva and Shakti. Everything that arises out of Consciousness is inherent within It, including Its own power of awareness and Its power to create.

Tantric texts then talk about the subtle body, the psychic mechanism, through which we have the capacity to perceive and understand the vital force and Consciousness within us. The psychic body is composed of our chakras, which are centers of awareness and energy. They must be awakened, so that we can experience the flow of vital energy that moves through us—a flow that is the resonance of all our chakras humming together in a state of openness.

Our physical body is the last structure of the four, and it correlates with the five elements of ether, air, fire, water, and earth. These are the lowest of the tattvas, the levels concerning the composition of matter. At the time of conception, the sushumna, the central channel of energy within us, begins to show itself as a streak of light in the womb. Everything in our body develops from this formless beginning. Once it manifests, the physical body is the densest form of consciousness within an individual, and is essentially "draped" over the psychic body. The physical body in itself has no consciousness; it is only infused with awareness from a subtler level. Therefore, when someone passes, their body is just inert matter, no different from a rock.

The physical body is the mirror that reflects back what is happening on a deeper level. Although trauma is physically held and felt in the body, in most cases the cause of the hurt isn't physical. Cancer, for example, is the result of trauma or tension creating a severe physical problem. From this perspective, even our emotions and thoughts are not held within the body; they are simply a reflection of a deeper state of resonance within us.

Our body serves as this reflective device, but as soon as the transmigratory soul leaves the body, it no longer remembers the physical. Of course, we should still take care of our body—as it is the vehicle we have been given for living—and that may include dealing with medical problems on the physical level, practicing yoga or sports, or engaging in expressive arts like dance. All of these things may help release some physical or emotional constraint.

The beautiful thing about the *Pratyabhijna Hrdayam* is that the sutras contain the wisdom of all the others within them. They all discuss how the unfoldment of the individual happens from within Pure Consciousness, and that is what is being described in this sutra. We see that manifestation is not a linear unfolding; it is a simultaneous matrix of creation without any disconnection between one part of existence and another. From this perspective, all four aspects of the human structure are equally important, and each is an expression of the unfolding of Consciousness. Although we can discuss the four levels in terms of energy that descends from the expanded state, the structure is not strictly hierarchical.

THE SOURCE OF THE PHYSICAL

This sutra helps us put into perspective how much we tend to focus on the physical body—and how that focus can be a distraction if we don't understand the source of the physical. The sutra also conveys that there is no death, because that which is alive is always alive. You are not your body; you do not die when your body fails. This in itself is a wonderful thing to know.

But this knowledge should also lead to freeing ourselves from the limitations of the body while we are alive. This is what is most important, because when we are established in that state of liberation, the causal body doesn't move forward and create another individuated body. We do not reincarnate, so no pranic, psychic, or physical body is needed. As the poet Kabir wrote:

> "Dying, dying, the world
> Is dying only.
> But lo! None knows how to die
> In such a way
> That he dies never again."

These four bodily structures are the encasements of Divine Consciousness. At the end of this lifetime, it is only the physical body that ceases to exist. The other three travel with us as we move from life to life. The consciousness that is the causal body is like a spaceship and the vital force in the subtle body captures all of our experience, including all of our patterns, tensions, and karma. We create karma as the result of our misunderstanding. It is the energy of self-serving willfulness and the action that springs from it.

All of that karmic debris is lodged in the chakras that constitute the psychic, or subtle, body. The central channel of that psychic body is the sushumna—which we can think of as a tube—and the impurities and karma are like sand clogging it up. Our entire psychic system is very much like the plumbing in a building. Over time, debris accumulates and the system gets stopped up, until eventually, very little water can move through the pipes.

These blockages create the *granthi*, the big boulders within the sushumna located in the base of the spine, the center of the heart, and the center of the head. They are the deep coalescence of our karma and trauma—like balls of string that keep getting bigger and bigger as we wind more layers on them. All of that accumulation is within the transmigratory soul. It is this density that blocks more and more of our life force, and we carry the same karma and limited understanding, no matter what body we manifest in.

CLEARING OUT INNER DENSITY

Each chakra either gets more clogged up, or is opened and expanded. There is energy and consciousness within each of our chakras that we release as we clean out the impurities, but from the Tantric perspective, realization does not happen until the granthi are dissolved. As the energy is freed, the first granthi to break open is the one in the base of the spine, followed by the heart, and finally the center of the head.

Granthi are like steel plates that prohibit the energy from rising back to the center of Consciousness, which is in the heart-space—the chakras in the heart, and in the center and top of the head. You can't call Roto-Rooter to go inside the sushumna and clear out the granthi because these knots have no manifest form. They only have a density of resonance from which patterns and tensions arise. When a granthi is dissolved, a major shift takes place, and that is usually the result of opening up inside while an intense contraction is happening.

Developing a deep inner flow of energy is so critical to our experience of awakening because it is the flow that washes away all the debris in us. It starts to penetrate through the density, creating enough of an opening that even more energy can move through our psychic body—and this progression continues until the flow pierces through within us and allows the Kundalini to rise up within that opening. This is why Kundalini Yoga, which focuses on raising the energy from the base of the spine to the top of the head, is the technique, the practice, and the experience that gives us our realization.

In my practice, we begin by opening our heart. That's where we start to get in contact with our Self. Then, we progressively bring our attention to breath, chakra, flow, and Presence. This is how Consciousness is revealed, although it's never a linear process. By consciously becoming aware of what is inside, developing and expanding the flow of energy within, we access our freedom. We are freed of all karma, all impurity, and all limited consciousness.

Although the physical body is the most condensed form of the four, it serves as the vehicle for our practice. Instead of filling our bodies with trauma, tension, drama, and self-rejection, let's use it for what it was intended—the means by which we engage day-to-day life experience to recognize our Divinity. There is no separation between anything in life. Even the body is the result of Supreme Consciousness. It is also the vessel that carries our own consciousness.

As we have discussed, there are many levels of perception within Consciousness. The last part of this sutra refers to what the Tantric texts call the "seven perceivers," which really means that there are seven levels of consciousness with differing capacities to perceive reality. If we multiply those seven by the five senses, we get the full range of perceptual ability—from Shiva Consciousness as the highest, all the way down to those forms of life that have a very limited capacity for experience.

All these levels of awareness are a reflection of the fact that the highest reality is hidden due to the contraction of Consciousness. As that contraction takes place, perception becomes denser and Consciousness has a diminished ability to see Itself. As human beings, we fall somewhere in that spectrum, but we have the opportunity to expand our awareness by focusing on the part of us that has never lost sight of Itself, even when we have become mired in contraction. Now and then clarity arises and we remember, if even for a moment, that we are not separate or different from Shiva.

Analyzing these levels of perception is just another angle of the prism, helping us see how everything that manifests is an aspect of the infinite unfolding into diversity, including our emergence as an individuated expression of the Divine Source.

RECOGNITION: BEING OBJECTIVE ABOUT OURSELVES

What is important about this sutra is that it allows us to step back and be more objective about ourselves and our understanding of why we have this life. This frees us from our attachment to our limited perspective. All this manifest complexity, all the sophistication of unfolding, is either our avenue to freedom or that which binds us.

When we get caught in the multiplicity it's as if we have tunnel vision. We see all the different elements within that complexity as distinct objects and we no longer perceive ourselves as the highest subject. Then, we get fixated on an object, and are locked in on something we think is outside ourselves. In that state, our consciousness diminishes and diminishes until we ultimately identify ourselves as an object, separate from the Supreme subject. The solution is to experience that the one Self has become "me" and lives day-to-day life for one purpose — to gain freedom.

तद्भूमिकाः सर्वदर्शनस्थितयः

tadbhūmikāḥ sarvadarśanasthitayaḥ

SUTRA EIGHT

The premises of all the systems of philosophy
are phases of this
(the structure of Consciousness).

Sutra Eight

Tantric practitioners of early times, just like everyone else, played politics. Perhaps there is a bit of arrogance showing in this sutra, because it implies that some *other* traditions don't really expound the highest perspective. Sutra Eight implies that other teachings do carry some truth but are an expression of a more limited understanding. This attitude is perhaps understandable if we place the *Pratyabhijna Hrdayam* in its historical setting, in a time when the exposition was part of a reaction against the prevailing Vedantic traditions.

The Vedantists did not hold the Tantic nondualistic view that both God and manifest creation are real. They believed the world was inherently an illusion that covered Consciousness, and this led to the idea that engagement with normal life carried a taint of impurity. Those practices therefore included rules requiring celibacy, vegetarianism, and other methods of living a "pure" life. The Tantrics vehemently rejected all such restrictions, instead emphasizing that engagement with the world is in fact necessary in order to integrate what we initially perceive as "inner" and "outer" reality.

All traditions come from Supreme Consciousness and reflect the level of unfolding of that Consciousness within them. The specifics of one tradition versus another are not the real point. The specifics are the diversity. Even within the three major schools of the Tantric tradition you will see apparent conflict, until you study them on a deeper level and realize that they are saying the same thing from their own perspective.

This sutra reminds us that all philosophical understanding — and in particular, our own philosophical understanding — is a perspective that is always based on how much Consciousness has revealed Itself within us. No understanding is bad, but whether it's our own beliefs or that of a traditional philosophy, it may be based on a limited unfolding of Consciousness.

For centuries people believed that if they sailed out across the ocean they would come to the edge of the world and fall off. That perspective greatly influenced life for a long time. Although we may now scoff at such ideas, for them it was totally real. It's like fear. Fear is real to each of us and it creates our life. It's all about perspective and our level of understanding.

RECOGNITION: TRANSCEND YOUR UNDERSTANDING

What I suggest is: Be very careful not to be attached to your own level of understanding. In particular, do not become very attached to any new level of belief or experience that arises due to spiritual practice. You will get it wrong. As soon as you think you have all the answers, you are putting another barrier in the way of your development. Once you are willing to admit that you don't know, you might begin to see.

It's critical to remember that any philosophy should be an explanation of experience, not a fixed perspective. Our experience will always be growing and therefore our perception of reality will shift. Don't get stuck in any level of experience. Seek the highest, and it will change your reality.

चिद्वत्तच्छक्तिसंकोचात्मलावृतः संसारी

cidvat tac chaktisaṃkocāt malāvṛtaḥ saṃsārī

SUTRA NINE

*That which possesses Consciousness,
through contraction of its powers
(becomes) a transmigratory individual
enveloped in impurities (the veils of duality).*

Sutra Nine

Here we see that Divine Consciousness, by Its own will, contracts to become the individual and covers it up with misunderstanding. In other words, God chooses to become us, but then He hides so well that we don't know our Source. We are enveloped within these "impurities," which is another way of saying that our perceptions are clouded by the veils of duality: I am separate, I am different, and I am the doer.

We become a transmigratory soul because we keep reinforcing our misunderstanding by repeating our patterns. We grind them into deeper and deeper grooves. This is the trap, but it is also the leverage point to spiritual freedom. Since we can choose to get off our self-created merry-go-round, we can let a different reality reveal itself to us: a Self that is not separate, not different, and is the true doer.

This is really good news, because karma is created by living in the veils of duality, and karma is the fuel of transmigratory souls. It is the energy that keeps re-creating this life and our destiny. Each of these veils reinforces the other, strengthening our experience of being bound by the experience of duality, lifetime after lifetime.

We create the direction and the destiny of our life based on the acts of self-absorption that arise from our misunderstanding. Rudi used to illustrate this point by telling a story. He suggested that if you drop a mouse into a bag of flour, it would eat its way out—but if you put a prize fighter into a man-sized bag, he would die of fright. The fighter would die from the fear of not being able to punch his way out, whereas the mouse, with no thought-constructs to bind him, would just accept the situation and eat his way out of it. When I say we create our own destiny, I don't mean whether someone grows up to be a shopkeeper or a CEO. Destiny refers to whether or not we achieve freedom. What other destiny is there, really?

SEPARATION VERSUS COMPLETENESS

The words "I am separate, I am different, and I am the doer" are a less personal way of saying, "I am self-absorbed." All of our acts of self-absorption and self-rejection are not separate. They are simply how our limited consciousness reinforces its own state. What happens when we function from the place of separation? We misunderstand and experience that we are imperfect and not whole. All of our striving, all of our reaching, and our incessant need to do something to fulfill ourselves is based on the misunderstanding of separateness. When we think, "I am separate," the natural belief that follows is, "There has to be something else that I need."

When we act from this place of lack, trying to fulfill some desire, we are simply reinforcing an endless cycle that is doomed to failure, because nothing outside us will ultimately provide completeness. Continually reaching for something from a sense of deficiency is a self-perpetuating consciousness that feeds upon itself. The transmigratory soul's vehicle has three engines. "I am separate" is one of those engines, and this misunderstanding is also the fuel that propels that experience of separateness out onto the horizontal. The result is that we find ourselves out of our center, fighting with our own self-rejection and self-absorption.

The only solution is to move back to center, and the first thing we need to do is to pull our awareness back inside. The second step is to detach, not only from the thought but from the feeling that has projected outward in the first place, giving rise to the form of the thought. Give your thoughts and emotions a lot less credence. Understand that they are not so real. Otherwise, what will happen is that although you take a breath and try to pull your energy inside, your mind will still be attached to the particular resonance that was fueling the projection. That only results in a tug-of-war, and whichever is stronger in any given moment wins—either your intention to move to center or your attachment to the projection.

At the core of this discussion is our need to surrender. Surrender is the key to discovering Unity. If we are trying to free ourselves from the grip of a mental projection, we must pull ourselves back and really let go of it. That projection was reinforcing a misunderstanding within us, so we have to be objective about our experience. Once we have taken a breath and detached from the mental construct that has created whatever we were attaching ourselves to, we have taken the energy out of that dynamic. We have absorbed it inside, into the flow, so that we can use the energy to expose a deeper consciousness.

You cannot be immersed in Unity when you are continually re-creating duality by being seduced by every emotion and every projection. So if a particular level of awareness is what made us reach outside ourselves, we pull ourselves out of that projection and find a deeper consciousness—one that does not need to reach or project because it is closer to understanding that it is whole in itself. In order to really transcend separateness we have to contact Unity. This is what gives us the strength to stay in our center, internalize our energy, and dissolve all separation.

HOW THE EGO RESISTS CHANGE

As we internalize our energy, the reality we create—from whatever level of misunderstanding of separation we function from—begins to dissolve. It no longer has the same power to reinforce itself. What does it feel like when your reality begins to get dissolved? Lighter, freer, as well as scary, painful, confusing, and ungrounded. All these types of experience are held within the same process of freeing ourselves from separateness. Usually what happens is that people begin to penetrate back into themselves and come to a place where a loss of the sense of separateness threatens something deep within them—their identity.

As we internalize our energy and begin to open inside, profound patterns of self-rejection and self-absorption are revealed. These patterns are like lions at the gate of each higher level of consciousness. The accumulation of lifetimes of tension and karma has a tremendous power to hold us within our ego, our limited awareness. These limitations are at the core of how our ego views itself. The ego seeks to protect its unconscious state, and it will fight back against emerging consciousness in order to maintain its separateness.

Our ego is a master at creating camouflage. As we penetrate deeper, become more awake inside, and there is the immanent possibility of a profound shift of consciousness, we subvert the process! The ego turns the energy outward and attaches it to something—usually to what somebody else did to us. Immediately, the incredible power of penetration, which was about to create a real transformation, gets diverted back outward into another, bigger, merry-go-round ride.

The distraction that subverts transformation does not have to take the form of a "negative" thought. When we are immersed in a stillpoint and begin to penetrate through the veil of separation, an impulse might arise that appears to be beautiful. Just as a leprechaun can trick us by changing its shape, the pulsation of spanda takes the form of something lovely and the energy of the thought takes our attention away from stillness, away from deepening ourselves further. So we have to let go of the thought and let go of the energy as it tries to re-form itself into something that is moving outward.

The moments that contain the greatest possibility of creating an internal shift require the most consciousness, the greatest stillness, and the deepest surrender. We have to be vigilant, because the veils of duality form a membrane like that of a very thin sheet of rubber. As we start to penetrate through it, the membrane expands and seems to get thinner—but right before we actually pierce the barrier, the pressure held in that space shoots us right back out. *What* reversed our direction and shot us back out is not relevant.

If we want to stop this reversal, we must discover stillness through our disciplined inner practice. When we are deeply silent but then start to feel some energy emerge, we bring our attention back to the subtlest breath, which brings us to a renewed experience of stillness. The moment we truly begin to penetrate through these veils is a pivot point in our meditation. You may experience an uncomfortable sense, almost a feeling of discombobulation, like being in two places at the same time. It can seem that way because your reality is shifting, and it isn't so firm. What we normally do then is start to rebuild a reality that we can feel secure about. But true surrender means being willing to let go of our reality—and if we can really do that, we will begin to penetrate the veils of duality and free ourselves of separation. We live in the illusion of maya, and because we cannot even see that we ourselves contracted the power of our own Divine Consciousness, we don't understand that we have a choice to change our experience. Our spiritual work is to actuate that choice.

EXPOSING OUR MISUNDERSTANDING

Every level of understanding needs to be surrendered; it doesn't matter what it is. All that we experience along the way to liberation is essentially just landscaping. Spiritual work is not about achieving anything. It is not about freeing ourselves from our imperfections—whatever they might be—but about revealing the part of us that is not imperfect. There is a critical difference between these perspectives. We are not fixing anything, because the part of us that re-creates reality, the karma that perpetuates the transmigratory soul, is an endless loop. We can't fix it from within itself but can only free ourselves *from* it. We can only free ourselves from the covering, the illusion, that *As the World Turns* is the totality of life.

All of our drama springs from the endless repetition of "I am separate." As we expose this misunderstanding it's important to avoid getting lost in the process itself. We do have to peel off all the layers of density within us, but it doesn't matter how many layers we have removed if we can't penetrate through the fundamental veil of separation that causes all misconception. So don't get lost in the details, but focus on really being able to surrender, so that when the innermost treasure is revealed, you are able to pierce through the final misunderstanding and become immersed in the underlying Unity.

Our inner core is like the epicenter of an earthquake, which shakes us on every level, including the surface of our daily lives. When we go through an emotional upheaval caused by what is happening to us, we are responding to the ripples of the shake, but that is not the same as being next to the epicenter. This is why we have to be more objective about our experience—to not get so caught up in the mundane superficiality of the experience of "I am separate"—and seek help to reach a deeper level. We can ask, "God help me free myself from my separateness."

Rudi explained that when we do penetrate into a deeper dimension of consciousness, a denser level of unconsciousness is also exposed. Every level of reality we find ourselves in is a concrete barrier we have to penetrate through in order to reach back into our Source. The closer we get to the primordial veil, "I am separate"—which is the strongest aspect of our experience— the more energy, strength, will, freedom, and surrender we have to bring to our work.

DISCOVERING THE DEEPEST LEVEL OF SELF

Sadhana is the discipline of discovering the deepest level of Self—although our transformation tends to happen slowly, over time. If our longing was powerful enough, we would be completely absorbed into Consciousness right away. We would pass quickly through every intervening level, because all density would simply dissolve in the intensity of our desire for freedom. But for most of us, it's necessary to find the Self again and again, until we have eventually burned away all barriers.

Our experience of distinction, of "I am different," limits the possibility of being immersed in Unity. If we continue to reinforce distinction and separation, that's the level of reality we re-create, moment by moment, in our lives. Every level of distinction is real. They are all too real. We can view the tattvas as a set of concentric circles, with "I am" being the Conscious center of all experience. The unfolding or densifying of Consciousness rolls out from there, but all of it is part of one whole. Your experience of being separate is real, as is that of being pissed off at somebody else—but these experiences function on different levels. Sadhana is about discovering the cause of suffering and freeing ourselves from that, rather than perpetuating the surface drama. We really need to be adults to do spiritual work.

What we are fundamentally detaching from is our limited understanding of life. Whether we see or experience something that is beautiful or not-so-beautiful, we have to penetrate through it to find its source. We have to discover the source of duality, which is Oneness, or Unity. If we are stuck in the perception of separation, we are still stuck, regardless of whether the surface experience is challenging or one that opens us. This happens when we look at other people and get caught in their form instead of seeing the Divinity and the beauty within them. Then we start to make distinctions and judgments: I am separate or different from them; I am better or worse than them.

When our individual consciousness forgets its Divine source, it gets confused and starts running in circles, becoming a transmigratory soul. We keep looking for something outside our Self because "I am separate" is experienced as, "I am not perfect and therefore I need something, and what I need is different than me." You must, and you will if you pursue your sadhana, free yourself from that misunderstanding. But you won't be able to do that if you continue to hold on to your attachment to separation, because every level of attachment is an expression of that. We have to accept the superficiality of our own consciousness and not seek to reinforce it.

THE LEVELS OF OUR LIFE

The activity we do in life is just part of the dance of creation. It's at the edge of the dance floor. Don't get so caught up in the details of the world or give them too much meaning. Our purpose in having this life has nothing to do with which career we are destined to have. The important thing we have to decide is whether to live inside or to lose contact with our Self when we project ourselves out into the world. We must look at our choices and ask: Do they support our underlying focus of finding our center?

So much of what we do on the surface level of diversity just doesn't impact the center. We have to merge the levels of our life and not get caught in some level of choice, thinking it is going to have a profound effect on our life experience—although it *does*, if we let our obsession with surface diversity distract us from our spiritual pursuit. The only way out is deeper in. Whatever misunderstanding of "out" we are experiencing is exactly the level of misunderstanding that we have to penetrate through. The details don't make a difference unless we get caught in them. As we move closer and closer to the point of surrendering our separate identity, we realize that our lives have simply been practice for that ultimate moment.

We have to experience the Oneness in all of the diversity. Along the way, there are no wrong choices in terms of how the details of life play out. Yes, there is some meaning in our work, and in who we choose as a partner, but the crux of the matter is whether we open our hearts and seek to understand a deeper reality. The only "wrong" choice is one that leads us to stop growing, to stop penetrating deeper inside because of some external experience. The things that show up in our lives and push our buttons are the very things we need to deal with in order to grow. Deal with that, so that you don't encounter the same irritant every time the merry-go-round goes by. Free yourself of your limited understanding instead of reinforcing it.

KARMA ARISES FROM MISUNDERSTANDING

Karma is another dynamic that arises from our misunderstanding. The first thing we must do is stop creating it. The next is to start burning it. We create karma *because* we are stuck in our limited perspective, but if we can penetrate through our misunderstanding our karma drops off. Most of us have to experience the reliving of some of our karma. The names and faces are changed to protect the guilty, but we relive the patterns of behavior, the ruts we have dug for ourselves. When our patterns show up right in front of us, then we must burn their energy instead of acting in a way that reinforces those patterns and creates new karma.

Nothing in our life is separate from us. The issue is what level of a particular karmic manifestation we choose to engage. Do we mistakenly see and engage it primarily as form and get caught in the specific dynamics of a situation, or can we penetrate beneath that and see our karma as energy repeating itself? But even when we see a situation in this light, we can either create a further repetition of karma with that energy, or we can free ourselves from it.

Our patterns do not show up to bind or constrict us but to free us. The deeper we are centered in ourselves, the earlier we can see a pattern of our karma starting to come our way. Then we can simply back away from it before the energy takes concrete form, before we react to it on the level of action. The point of living in stillness is that we don't reengage the energy.

It's not simply a matter of knowing whether an action will or will not create more karma, because karma is only one of the binding effects of misunderstanding. A more fundamental misunderstanding is that we think we are the doer, and it is doing *itself* that creates karma. Doing comes from the reinforcing of some incomplete part of ourselves. We have a sense of needing something and therefore feel we have to do something to fill that need. Anytime we need something, we become attached to an outcome.

We are seeking to transform the belief that any thing or experience is outside of us and that we are the doer. The only doer is Divine Consciousness. Everything unfolds from within That, never separate from That, even as It creates an incredible display of diversity and experience. The human bandwidth usually encompasses only a very limited range of possibility. Even when we speak of "seeing the Divinity in others," we are displaying the misunderstanding that there is an "other" that is separate from us. We must see the Divinity in ourselves, and then we will see it everywhere, without separation and without the belief that only some things are beautiful and Divine.

It is solely by penetrating into the source of all life that we really understand Unity. Otherwise, we will always be trying to understand universal awareness through a limited lens. We must be willing to surrender our limited perspective about the very viewpoint we function from. The totality of every experience of life and death on earth is still a very thin band, relative to the realm of manifest Consciousness. From God's perspective, earth is a speck on a speck on a speck, no more or less important than the other specks. Only we insist on overinflating our experiences—evaluating whether the minutia of life is good or bad—when the highest reality is that all of life is an expression of the Divine's choice to manifest for the sheer joy of it.

If everything unfolds for that one simple purpose of expressing joy, then everything that unfolds is contained within that purpose. We think we are born, live, do, and die, and therefore we believe we have control over life. Who has control over when they are born or die? Only a person who is free from the cycle of birth and death has any choice in those matters, and if we don't have control over those two things, we probably don't have much control over what happens in between. What we do have control over is our capacity to be aware.

When we talk about opening and growing, it is in the context of using our free will to follow either the expansion or contraction of Consciousness. We *can* choose not to grow. Isn't that interesting? Even within the one Divine Will, which is to create the expansion of the joy of Consciousness, we have the power to accept or reject the Grace that is offered to us. Grace continually rains down on us, but if we don't confer Grace on God, then His Grace can't reach us. This is the extraordinary power of the ego—the place that we say is limited—that it can reject the unlimited.

RECOGNITION: OFFERING OURSELVES TO GOD

God created this world, and we have our own world that we get to create within it. Everything has perfection within itself, but when we don't perceive on that level we can get contracted over something and label it "bad." All of life is here to teach us about our limited understanding. The perfect contraction is the very thing that frees us from our misunderstanding. Even our fears have profound value if we get beyond going around and around in a circle with them. We can choose to penetrate beneath the surface and recognize the source of our fear, and then the source of the next level of fear.

We have to get beyond our understanding and beliefs about our world. It is only in the surrendering of those things that some deeper truth reveals itself. You can think of each level of awareness as having a steel barrier above and below it, and what happens on that level just bounces like a ball between the top and bottom. Every level of life is real, but each has a ceiling and a floor of consciousness within it. Surrender is the only means of penetrating through those boundaries. That is why surrender is the key to freedom.

We have to surrender our experience of separateness, of being different, and, most importantly, the sense that we are doing. All of us can perhaps conceptually conceive that "I am not separate, and I am not different," but very few can really understand, "I am not doing anything." The first step to experiencing not doing is to say, "God, do it for me." Offer yourself into that. Ask, "God, show me my life," and *mean* it—and then, when something immediately shows up that doesn't happen to look the way you think God *ought* to have designed it, surrender again. Ask and ye shall receive. But don't have a checklist in hand. Don't ask, "Please give me my life and make sure it includes this, and this, and this, and I am sure you must have a returns policy."

There is nothing happening in our lives that is not happening from within us. We have to fully engage in that unfolding, and the first step is to create a horizontal flow with our life instead of rejecting it. As we begin to create this flow, we are establishing a give and a take, reabsorbing our experience back into ourselves, refining it, and hopefully then projecting out a higher experience. That flow is an engagement with the power of Consciousness to create, to express. The life that is manifest on the screen of our consciousness is now expressed from a deeper state of awareness.

Everything that happens in our life is an expression of perfection, of Shiva's desire to make Himself bigger, just for the fun of it. In the process of manifesting the universe, He probably has a pretty good flow with it, and because of that, has even more energy to create.

Ask that you may be complete. Ask, "May my will be Your will." It would be incredibly powerful if that was your mantra, instead of, "God give me this . . . God give me that . . . God free me from what I don't like in my life." From my experience, the highest expression of our will is to surrender it. How prepared are you to surrender your will? How willing are you? How do you think this would affect your experience?

We have to be careful, however, that when we offer ourselves to God's will, we are not also perpetuating the subtle thought, ". . . and if I do that, then life is going to be exactly the way I want it to be." If we wish to truly surrender, we have to trust God. In reality, Shiva is already doing everything, not even through us but as us. It is only being caught in the veil of separation that makes us think we are in charge, and the veils are extremely subtle. Even our wish to grow must ultimately be surrendered, because at some point we have to let go of the idea that it is *we* who are doing the wishing. It is only God doing the wishing.

तथापि तद्वत्पञ्चकृत्यानि करोति

tathāpi tadvat pañcakṛtyāni karoti

SUTRA TEN

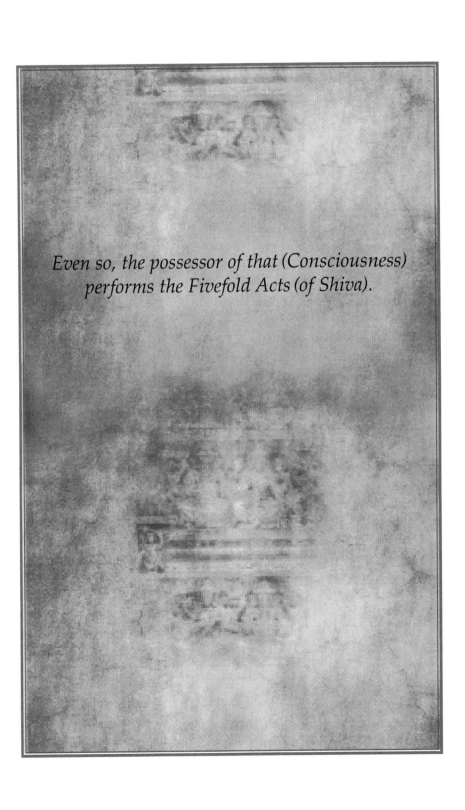

Even so, the possessor of that (Consciousness) performs the Fivefold Acts (of Shiva).

Sutra Ten

As we have mentioned, the Fivefold Acts of the Divine are creation, maintenance, dissolution, concealment, and revelation. We are all born, we live for a while, and then we die. The first three acts are happening all the time, but what determines our experience of them is whether our consciousness is expanding or contracting. In other words, the fundamental choice we have is whether to stay on life's merry-go-round—which conceals our true nature—or to focus on revealing our higher Self. If we don't make a conscious effort to reveal this inner reality, transmigration continues to happen, lifetime after lifetime, from one merry-go-round to the next.

Concealment started at tattva 6, with the advent of maya. This is when the illusion of our separation arose, when our true Divine nature was obscured. Grace is the antidote to concealment, and we can experience this force in our own life, opening our awareness back to our Source. Unfortunately, we can also witness what happens in the lives of people, who, for whatever reason, haven't had the possibility of a profound spiritual realization exposed within them.

The level of concealing or revealing in each person's life is based on their karma. What arises in any lifetime is always the result of whether concealing was previously reinforced or whether there was some unfoldment of higher awareness. At any time the Grace of Consciousness can arise within us, calling forth the understanding that we can transcend concealment.

If that act of revelation doesn't happen, then we perpetuate the transmigratory cycle of being born, living, and dying. We continue to misunderstand and live in the veils of duality. Grace comes along for one reason: not to make our lives easier or more fun, but to reveal to us our misunderstanding and free us from all separation. Grace doesn't care whether our lives change. It cares whether our *experience* of life changes, regardless of our circumstances.

WE MASK OUR TRUE SELF

These Fivefold Acts are continually happening, from the highest Consciousness of Shiva to, and through, our individuated consciousness. It is through our own actions that we mask our true Self, or at least maintain the concealment. In a sense, we are co-conspirators with God. He set concealment in motion, but it is our own misunderstanding that continues to hide the truth. More specifically, it is our attachment to our limited understanding that conceals the truth.

Why are we so attached to our own level of understanding? That is how separateness maintains itself, and the ego has a vested interest in maintaining the status quo. The aim of the *Pratyabhijna Hrdayam,* and of all the ancient Tantric texts, is to focus us on piercing the veils of duality—and that will shatter everything you think you know. If it doesn't, you aren't piercing duality. In order to pass through this remarkable transformation, we must trust that there is an intelligence greater than our own. There is a beautiful saying in Proverbs, "Trust in the Lord with all your heart; and don't lean on your own understanding. In all things acknowledge Him, and He shall direct your way."

When we watch birds flying we can imagine how wonderful that would be, and yet we are afraid to soar. It is ironic that we perpetuate concealment. For some reason, we think that maintaining our separate identity is a good thing. We cling to the theory that at some point our life will be really fabulous, despite the fact that all of our experience to date has demonstrated that separation leads to endless suffering. We steadfastly believe that as soon as we change life's conditions enough, all will be well.

The primary glue of our own concealment is always our limited perception and consciousness, and the patterns and tensions that are created from within those limitations. Added to this is our incessant demand that life should give us something other than what has been given. We display a basic unwillingness to serve that which gave us life, instead of honoring our Source with all of our actions. This is part of the reason we don't fly.

The other thing that keeps us earthbound is holding on to our will—being unwilling to surrender to a higher Consciousness. This is essentially insisting, "My consciousness is higher than God's. I know better." This basic unwillingness to surrender our separateness and our will has only one result: The experience we have is the one we create. It's also the experience we *want*, because if we truly desired something better, we would be willing to let go. Ain't that a bitch? We can't blame anybody else. We can't do anything but deeply recognize that maintaining concealment is our own act.

GRACE DISPELLS CONCEALMENT

In one sense we are doing exactly what God is doing, yet there is a fundamental difference in experience. God is going through His Fivefold Acts having a terrific time. We, too, are going through them but often suffer, because we are caught in act four, concealment. Part of the power of that obscuration is that we don't even realize that there is a fifth act of revelation. Not only does act four hide our true nature, it covers up the fact that we even *have* a true nature! But then, by an act of Grace, the Divine gives us a fragrance, a whisper, an initial pulsation that starts to reveal the inadequacy and the consequences of concealment.

This Grace arises from within us. Everything from that moment on is the expansion of that revelation, the expansion of Grace—including meeting a teacher to further guide us. From the very initial pulsation of Grace, revelation continues because we open to it and ask for it to grow. Conversely, revelation can become submerged if we refuse to accept and open to it. Our will and our ego can be so strong that we even submerge God within us. We can suppress this act of Grace that's trying to open us. We have that power.

The revelation that begins to bubble up from within us is what we must respond to, and the moment we truly feel God's Grace is something we will never forget. My own life is an example of this. I was raised a Methodist and then became an atheist. As a teen, I was caught in my own confusion, leaning on my belief that there was no Divinity, and—truth be told—I had not much hope in life. Then suddenly, one day all I could think about was God, and shortly after that I heard about my teacher. That 180-degree turn was certainly a moment of Grace, but I am continually grateful that I have been able to respond to that moment throughout the rest of my life.

Sometimes, even as we are responding to Grace, we still get caught in our patterns and tensions, and we have to find our way back again. Concealment may hide revelation for a while. That's not an issue. The real issue is whether we deeply understand and feel gratitude for the Grace that is being offered in our life. Gratitude is something we must consciously cultivate in every moment, not just when we think life looks good or is happening as we would choose. Quite the contrary: Be grateful for the times you are challenged, because this is when real change is possible.

Just as the manifest universe is Shiva's act of concealment, your universe in all its diversity is your own act of concealment. But remember, Shiva hid Himself because it is only through concealment that revelation happens. If we don't understand that God's purpose is to once again reveal this Source, we get caught on the horizontal and in the circular process of life. We keep trying to force life to change on that surface level in order for our experience to change. Real transformation requires something completely different: that we stay in our center, be still, and watch as Shiva unfolds the Grace of our lives. That would be pretty amazing.

FOCUSING ON REVELATION

If we bring consciousness to the first three of the Fivefold Acts in our lives, we bring meaning to whatever is happening in our lives. But there is a critical distinction here: We must infuse life with meaning instead of trying to extract meaning from life. Our lives are the stage upon which these five acts are performed. In fact, we are simultaneously the player, the audience, and the scriptwriter. The recognition of the oneness of these roles is sometimes called "witness consciousness." In this state we have the ability to watch our lives with some objectivity and nonattachment to our own perspective. When we have this clarity we see that it is by giving so much meaning to all the minute details of life that we conceal our own true and highest nature. It's not that the details don't have meaning; it's just that they are not as important or meaningful as we think they are. We give the details so much meaning that they obscure our own highest Consciousness.

We repeat these Fivefold Acts in every moment, throughout our lives. The key is to focus on act five. Bring consciousness into the cycle you are repeating and know that the other four acts are all part of the process of revealing. Understand the cycle from this perspective. The ability to choose is a power we have within our own lives, given to us by the highest power. It's not practical, or even logical, to choose anything but revealing, yet we continually choose concealment. Why? Because we live in our egos and that is what the ego does. This is why we have to free ourselves from the grip of the ego and from the veils of duality, which are the source of the ego's power.

Grace, the act of revelation, is constantly raining down on us, but we prefer to walk around under an umbrella. We even share that umbrella with our friends! Each of us must choose to let Grace penetrate into our lives. We must focus on Grace and revelation and surrender everything that gets in the way of that opening. Surrender means letting go of whatever we hold on to when revelation begins to unfurl in us, as it threatens to really change us. When you do feel threatened by change, be still and don't react. Just surrender and commit to letting go of your limited self.

We take life moment by moment, and every time something difficult arises, that's the opportunity to choose revelation instead of concealment. Typically, we justify our concealment by thinking, "I'm not ready; I'm not there yet." That's bullshit: If it's there in your face, it's trying to wake you up. How can you say that you are not there yet? Remember, everything happens from within us, for the purpose of our liberation. It's like setting the alarm for six in the morning, and when it rings to wake us up, we insist that it isn't six o'clock yet. Really? The alarm has gone off. We don't get to choose when, we only get to choose if we open or if we close. Surrender isn't something that happens later, when we have become more capable of letting go. The time to surrender is now. This is important to remember, because we can perpetuate the transmigratory experience forever, if we choose to do so.

Grace is the freedom-bestowing power of the Divine. It exists to enable Shiva to remember Himself after He concealed Himself by manifesting the universe. So this is not our process. This is Shiva's process, and it just happens to be played out through us, as us. Whatever we think is limiting us is in truth trying to free us. You will not always understand Grace or what It is trying to unfold in you. What you can always do is ask It to unfold unconditionally, instead of rejecting and fighting against It.

My own experience is that when Grace appeared in my life, It was not always in a form I imagined or even desired. For fifteen years I managed a food-service business owned by the ashram I lived in—and that meant working seven days a week, sixteen hours a day. I had to penetrate through the surface hardship and the resentment that threatened to arise whenever my responsibilities kept me from having more interaction with my teacher or from being able to go on group travels abroad. I did my work because I understood the Grace of having to overcome all my projections, all my attachments, and all my misunderstanding about who I was.

We have to surrender and burn through every limitation in ourselves, every part of us that rebels against what life is trying to show us. The purpose of Grace is to reveal; not to confirm what we know but to reveal what we don't know. Growth is an organic process, and the depth of our wish is what determines how long or how fast transformation takes. You cannot imagine or even understand the challenge to your identity that you will face as you move into your spiritual Self. If you knew in advance, you would stay in act four forever! It is a lot easier to not know what you are going to face. The only solution is to live in a place of openness, stillness, and surrender. Selflessly serve, and selfless receive the Grace that has appeared in your life.

RECOGNITION: THE ESSENTIAL CHOICE

We exist in individuated form because Shiva concealed Himself. When he chose to manifest as the entirety of creation, he valued the experience of his inherent state so much that he imagined that it would be wonderful to forget Himself in that creation, for the sheer joy of remembering again, and that is the force of revelation. Because we are not separate from that infinite, radiant Source, we perform the same Fivefold Acts as He does, with every breath of our life. We can get lost in the endless cycle of creation, maintenance, and dissolution, thereby concealing the higher awareness available within that manifestation. Or, we can choose to use our capacity for self-awareness to tune in to that which will reveal the Source of our life. The choice is whether we live in the pain of the concealment of our highest Self, or in the joy of remembering.

Consciousness has within Itself the two aspects of being the substance and the illuminating power of life, and having the capacity to be aware of Itself—to be aware that It *is* illuminating life. That self-referential capacity to be aware is the gift of Grace. For those of us fortunate enough to be engaged in sadhana, a spiritual force emerges from within our deepest Self—cracking the concrete encasing our heart, letting out that illuminating power. This is the light of Grace, the force of revelation.

Divine Grace may come like a bolt of lightning, but it is our responsibility to accept It and allow It to free us. To *beg* Grace to free us. This is how we take responsibility for ourselves and make the choice to live in liberation, in a state of profound joy.

आभासनरक्तिविमर्शनबीजावस्थापन-
विलापनतस्तानि

ābhāsanaraktivimarśanabījāvasthāpana-
vilāpanatas tāni

These (i.e., the Fivefold Acts of Shiva) take place in the individual as illuminating (the object), fixing our awareness in it, understanding it, (thus) planting a seed (of limitation), and releasing (that misunderstanding).

Sutra Eleven

Here we have a further elaboration of the Fivefold Acts—describing how we give life to objects by illuminating them, and how we then interact with those objects by enjoying and knowing them. What is particularly interesting is that as we do that, we are also planting seeds of limiting memories, called *samskaras*, the residue of the actions of our life. We move through life functioning from these deep impressions that are stored in our subtle physiology, and this is another way we engage in the act of concealment.

Objects are like a first teenage crush: all-engrossing in the moment, perhaps painful to let go of, but then quickly forgotten. Just like a boyfriend or girlfriend is no longer in our awareness three months after our parents broke us up by moving to a new town, when we withdraw our attention from the object, it just disappears. This is a powerful example of what we do with our mind all the time.

When we are attached to objects in this way, we function from a place of misunderstanding rather than from the highest place possible for us. We can only give up our attachments when we consciously choose to let go of the part of us that is rooted in separation and holds on from there. As we choose to find understanding and higher awareness within us, nonattachment is the natural expression of making contact with and becoming established in that state. It is never, ever a rejection of anything.

Learning to live in the effulgent simplicity of desirelessness is the discovery of that place within where attachment is not even an issue, because we perceive the nature of the world and feel complete in that Unity.

Consciousness is the field and the Source of everything, and creation is the manifestation that happens from the power within that. So from within Itself the ongoing cycles of creation, maintenance, and dissolution arise and fall. The issue is always whether we are conscious of what is happening in that particular cycle: whether that unfolding of creation conceals or reveals its own source. Manifest form appears solid, but in reality it is only the condensation of Consciousness, Shiva concealing Himself in what He created. In the merging of subject and object, we find the underlying Unity.

RECOGNITION: EVERYTHING IS WITHIN YOU

The desire to know and to live as God is never the attempt to find something outside of ourselves. It is only discovering that which already exists within us. All other desires are the reaching for happiness in something other, but we know that those things we seek to make us happy generally have the opposite effect. In fact, it is this relentless search that is the true cause of our unhappiness.

There is tremendous power in the attachment we create to the very objects that arise from within us. This is concealment. We create something, it has some duration of life, and then it goes away, but in the process we conceal what it really is. Fortunately, we can also choose to dissolve that concealment. Our experience tells us that we enjoy and maintain objects, but as soon as we disengage our awareness from them, they dissolve.

From a state of deep internal quietness, you must ask yourself what you truly want in this life. Do you want to be happy or unhappy for the rest of your life? It's unfortunately a fact that most people function from unhappiness — from the consciousness of suffering — instead of living in the consciousness of freedom, in the effulgent simplicity and joy that is always available to us. If we are willing and choose to discover it, this consciousness saturates the rest of our life.

तदपरिज्ञाने स्वशक्तिभिर्व्यामोहितता
संसारित्वम्

tadaparijñāne svaśaktibhir
vyāmohitatā saṃsāritvam

SUTRA TWELVE

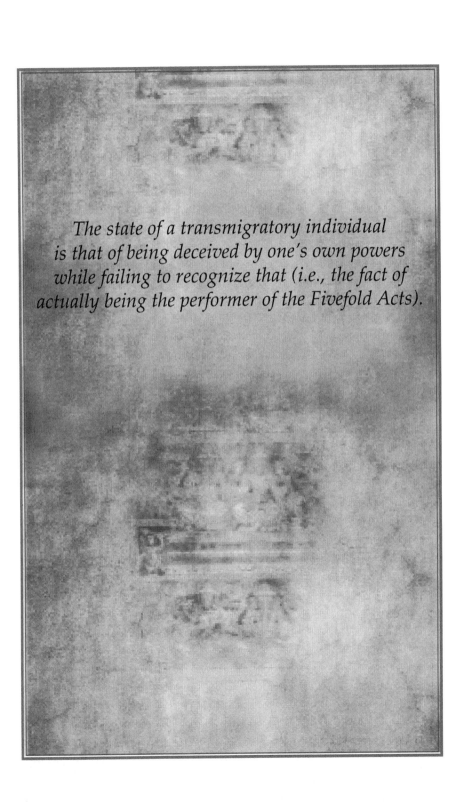

*The state of a transmigratory individual
is that of being deceived by one's own powers
while failing to recognize that (i.e., the fact of
actually being the performer of the Fivefold Acts).*

Sutra Twelve

Once again, the message is that we mistakenly think we are the doer. While it is true that the Fivefold Acts happen in our individuated life, the source, field, and energy of our actions are simply Shiva being engaged in *His* Fivefold Acts. When we don't recognize that Shiva is the only real doer, we get confused. Then, we believe that we are in control of life, and we attempt to control everyone in our life in order to influence what happens to us. This only perpetuates the misunderstanding that we need something outside ourselves to be complete.

It says in the Bhagavad Gita, "Surrender all action to Me, with the mind resting on the highest Self, freed from desire and the sense of mind, abandon that you are the doer." When Shiva is perceived as the doer, our experience radically changes. Shiva knows He's not separate or different—because He created everything from within Himself. When we surrender to Shiva as the only doer, there is no longer any struggle. We live in bliss, which is the unbounded joy of experiencing our own existence.

How many of us function in that state within ourselves? Not many. Unfortunately, our usual experience of our own existence is laced with suffering. Why would we choose to remain in suffering? Understand that on the other side of the door named Surrender is the unconditional, unbounded joy of existence. We have to merge into Shiva to walk through that door, and the key to the door is giving up the illusion that we are a separate individual who is doing something.

Even the breath within us is not our own. We think we have to breathe to be alive, but in reality, we don't even perform that action. Breath is simply the pulsation of God within us. He is breathing us, and the sound of that breathing is "Aham," Shiva endlessly repeating, "I am." This internal breath is how God sustains our very existence, from within Himself.

THE ARISING AND SUBSIDING OF THOUGHT AND EMOTION

We are engaging in the Fivefold Acts all the time, even in our thinking process. The question is, which act are we aware of and functioning from? The *Spandakarikas* discuss how a subtle energetic pulsation gives rise to a thought, which has some duration, and then subsides. Or rather, that is what would happen if we were not attached to our thoughts. Because we are attached, thoughts start to confuse and bind us, and they conceal. If we can find our center again and penetrate to the source of a thought, revelation can take place.

We may find this internal stillpoint during meditation, but when we get up off our cushion, the mind starts to engage again. Mental activity becomes a problem only when it pulls us out of stillness, out of that deeper consciousness within. Losing our center often happens because we believe we have to act on our thoughts—a natural result of thinking we have to *do* something to make our lives better. If we can remain still and rest in the awareness that we are not the doer, we can carry revelation out into our daily lives.

The same principle applies to our emotions. They are powerful and they will grip us. But when we develop the capacity to watch an emotion come up without getting sucked into its vortex, it too just arises and subsides. We can, through our detachment, recognize that the arising and subsiding is just an ongoing process, and not give the emotion so much validity.

We have then revealed the limiting quality of emotions. We have all had the experience that any given feeling can be either all-consuming or as small and insignificant as a gnat. The further an emotion pulls us out from our center, the more work we have to do to pull ourselves back to the inner place from which we can recognize that the emotion wasn't as valid as we thought it was.

Every time we forget and think that we are the doer we get attached to our thoughts and emotions. As a result, we get caught up in our patterns and tensions, and we fight to prove ourselves right. We are unwilling to surrender our perspective—and the ultimate perspective is our belief that we are doing something. We have to learn to trust God, and surrender reflects this trust. It allows us to let go of our perspective and the need to control, because deep inside we know that life is expressing itself perfectly, as it is. Surrender is the recognition of that perfection, and the surrendering to God's process. It is surrendering to Shiva's will, the perpetual expansion of freedom.

This entire discussion of the Fivefold Acts reminds us that not only do we have a choice about how we experience life, we must consciously exercise that choice. We have the capacity to be aware of ourselves, and that includes the ability to choose our experience by choosing to keep our attention in our center. The expression "lost in thought" literally describes what happens to us if we are immersed in concealment. The Fivefold Acts are the process of revealing the highest truth, that everything is an expression of the field of Consciousness.

RECOGNITION: LET YOUR LIFE REVEAL ITSELF

What is your purpose in life? Holding on to your limitations, or focusing on your ability to free yourself of them? Most people walk through life in a stupor, in concealment, and aren't aware that they have the choice to try to change their perception—and so they don't. Sometimes we try to change our awareness and we don't quite accomplish it. Don't worry, the same dynamic will come back around, until you are able to open and change.

It's only our misperception that anything in our life is inherently negative. It's only negative if we contract. If we get bigger, it is positive. Penetrating through duality is what really changes our perspective. We must stop thinking that our environment is separate from us. Every struggle is a test of what you are really committed to; it demonstrates what you actually want, regardless of what you say you want. There is this tug-of-war between life trying to pull you out of your center and you trying to pull back in. Rudi said that a developed capacity is a muscle system, and we need a strong one to win the game.

When we are not fully aware that everything is happening because of Shiva, then we remain confused. Once we do understand that we were never in control, we stop trying to have control—which never managed to fulfill us, no matter how hard we tried to manipulate life. If we really want to be free from the veils of duality we must let our life reveal itself. The willingness to surrender control is the means to understanding that we are not the doer. And just when we think we have given up control, we find out that we haven't. Truly letting go will rip you apart and it will free you. Eventually, you will understand that your life is not about you.

तत्परिज्ञाने चित्तमेव अन्तर्मुखीभावेन
चेतनपदाध्यारोहात्चिति:

tatparijñāne cittam eva antarmukhībhāvena
cetanapadādhyārohāt citiḥ

SUTRA THIRTEEN
AND THE UPAYAS

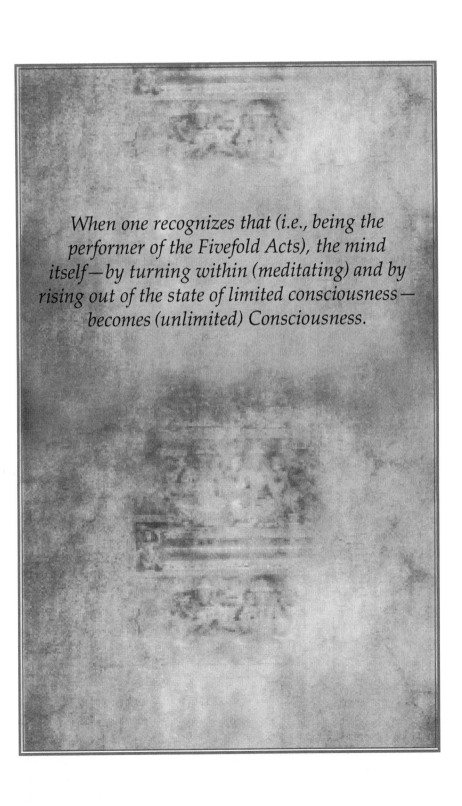

When one recognizes that (i.e., being the performer of the Fivefold Acts), the mind itself—by turning within (meditating) and by rising out of the state of limited consciousness—becomes (unlimited) Consciousness.

Sutra Thirteen and the Upayas

As we have discussed, a significant theme in the *Pratyabhijna Hrdayam* is the elaboration of how Consciousness descends from Its expanded state, condensing into more limited consciousness. Human beings are an expression of that descent of Consciousness from Unity to duality and then into all the diversity of existence. Arising at the level of tattva 12, we are an individuated embodiment of the Divine whole—but we have seen that shortly after this juncture, Consciousness further descends from Its expanded state to the point where It becomes mind.

The sutras go on to describe the effect of having the limited awareness that we experience through our mind. However, in Sutra Thirteen, something new is suggested: The process of descending into more limited consciousness can be reversed. In recognizing the fact that we are Shiva performing the Fivefold Acts, we can gain a new awareness and the mind itself can become Consciousness. I love this, because inherent in this statement is that the mind isn't conscious, yet it can *become* conscious. When the mind opens back up and tunes in to its source, its own nature, we start to understand the higher truths of life.

SEEING A DEEPER REALITY

In the previous sutras we were beginning to glimpse that God lives as us, and that we are not the doer. When we see this reality,

171

all of a sudden the mind shifts and starts to move back toward its own source, to expand into Divine Consciousness. It does this by rising to the state of full expansion through meditation, which is the tuning of our awareness inside. As we get still and feel into the bindu point of that single Consciousness, then our consciousness expands instead of descending further into obscuration.

The mind changes its gaze. Instead of looking out, it begins to look in. As we discussed, our experience of life is totally determined by whether the highest Consciousness within us is revealing or concealing Itself. By tuning within we begin to break the grip of the veils of duality. The most important change is that we surrender the delusion and the illusion that we are in control, or that we are doing anything. This is the pin that pops the bubble of duality. In our search for Oneness, what is revealed is that all of diversity is simply the dance of Shiva.

This sutra says that a major transformation happens when the mind begins to turn within. Here is the introduction of sadhana, the work we must do to allow our consciousness to expand beyond its limitation and return to the unbounded state. We have seen that unlimited Consciousness, as it condenses, becomes limited mind. When we start to find and tune in to a place of limitless awareness within, we come to understand that we are Shiva and Shakti's dance. It is the surrender into something bigger that allows the mind to expand again.

The mind doesn't dissolve—it expands—although you could say that its *boundaries* are dissolved. Once the mind is free from the boundary of limited understanding, it is no longer mind; it is expanded Consciousness. Then, our awareness is focused on our Self, on the recognition of our Source. This process begins on our cushion as we meditate, but sadhana must extend into every aspect of our lives or it is not real.

THE UPAYAS

A discussion of the *upayas* is useful at this point, because they describe the matrix of how we engage in spiritual practice. *Upaya* translates as "the means to realization." Each upaya conveys a different aspect of focusing our consciousness back to its highest Self. As we move through this progression of means, we see how our experience shifts from an experience of duality to one of Unity. The upayas are directly related to the process of allowing the Kundalini to rise, eat through, and dissolve the tensions and knots in our psychic system. The upayas are:

- *Anavopaya* – the path of effort

- *Shaktopaya* – the path of energy

- *Shambhavopaya* – the path of awareness

- *Anupaya* – no path, simply living as God

Depending on the level of our own consciousness at the particular moment we begin to wake up, some of those upayas may be the predominant strategy that we utilize on ourself. Just like the tattvas and the sutras, our work is never linear. We don't graduate from anavopaya, get a diploma, and then go on to shaktopaya. All of the upayas function at the same time, but there is a predominance of awareness about what we are doing and where we are doing it from.

Anavopaya is the effort to meditate, the effort to create a disciplined inner practice and to learn to serve. Traditionally, when a person came to a guru, the teacher required that the potential student work and do service for twelve years. They went to the fields and dug. This was primarily done so that students could to prove to themselves how serious they were about what they said they wanted. It was a process of learning how to deeply surrender, regardless of what was required.

These days we get to meditate right away, but the effort is still one of developing discipline. This is foundational. Without a regular practice, we don't progress. The fundamental thing we start with is finding a true wish to grow. The essence of anavopaya is developing that wish, which includes not dictating *how* we grow. It looks like we are still doing in the world, but we are beginning to turn our attention inside and to surrender to the unfolding of a higher force. This work allows us to really break down the grossest level of our ego, the wall that initially prevents us from getting inside and keeps us separate from the experience of Unity.

At the same time, we engage in shaktopaya by recognizing that life is energy. We incorporate that awareness into our disciplined inner practice by establishing a flow in ourselves. This is how we come to experience spiritual energy moving through our psychic body. We also understand that shaktopaya is the transformation of the energy of the mind into higher consciousness.

In our practice we talk about the progression of experience as breath, chakra, flow, and Presence. Living in Presence is a good way of describing shambhavopaya. Entering into that state happens through the sadhana of anavopaya and shaktopaya. In rare cases, a person may find themselves at that threshold as the result of their spiritual growth in past lives. In either case, the person has developed a true awareness of their own source in Consciousness, and the energy itself upholds Presence.

Anupaya is the means by which our individuality is instantly dissolved by Divine Grace. In one moment of receiving *shaktipat* (the descent of Grace), with one glance or word from the guru, we recognize our highest Self in a flash. Anupaya does not require meditation or service. There is no path at all at this point, because we are directly experiencing "I am Shiva." Once that happens, Shiva is the only doer and there is nothing for the sadhaka to do. This is the highest of the upayas, but it is only the experience of very few individuals.

AN INTEGRATED APPROACH TO SPIRITUAL WORK

We can understand the upayas as being part of the balance within us. Different times in our life require different means of focusing our consciousness. It's a bit like playing tennis. Sometimes you need to hit the ball hard and deep, and sometimes you just finesse it over the net. How do we know which to do? We are aware. We play with our eyes open and evaluate the need of the moment. The same ability applies to our lives. Because we are aware, we can decide what we need to do.

My teacher Rudi was a perfect example of all the upayas functioning at once. He told us to work—and we did that at every level. It's never that we stop doing one thing. We're like a short-order cook handling multiple dishes in various stages of preparation. We attend to it all, and every type of work continues throughout our sadhana. The first instruction I give students is, "Open your heart," because our heart is the doorway to God. That is where we feel God's Presence, in a state of openness. Although Presence is immediately apparent in our practice, every type of work we do is to allow that Presence to grow bigger, until we fully merge with God. Although there isn't a strictly linear progression to our work, there is some element of linearity because our own consciousness is being refined over time.

The path of effort is never completely left behind. Even after we are established in a profound, deep state of Presence there will be times when we have to work. Perhaps we discover that the state of surrender we live in is not as profound as we believed it to be. Or the veils of duality we thought we had pierced through all of a sudden begin to cover us again. At such times, we have to be proactive and work deeply inside, but work from a different state, from being established in Presence. It is just a different type of work. You could say that *what* is working is different. When we live in a state of Presence, Shiva does all the work.

For most people, the impulse to "do" comes from the need to have something that will complete themselves. As we have discussed, we only think we have to complete ourselves because we feel separate and therefore incomplete. By not reaching, by being still and open, by receiving and giving from exactly where we are, we establish ourselves in true surrender. This is our means to freedom from the veil of duality that leads us to think we are doing anything. We all live amidst a magnificence that is unfolding at every moment. Just because we stop doing things doesn't mean something isn't getting done, or that there isn't a higher power doing everything.

The matrix of understanding and sadhana intersect and support each other. This is why the upayas are part of the discussion of these sutras. The upayas describe the nature of how we turn our awareness back inside. We refocus our consciousness away from the mind and senses—which are how we create our external world—back to the Source of the external. This is how we begin to pierce duality and see that diversity is not something separate but simply the effect of our own consciousness.

When we turn our awareness within, the mind itself becomes Consciousness. Just a few sutras back the text was about Consciousness becoming the mind, but now, revealing is starting to happen. Concealing is no longer the only force operating, even though it is still a factor in our experience. It takes a lot of time to shine the light so that we can see everything, and the upayas describe how the mind is transformed, how higher Consciousness unfolds as we tune in to a deeper and deeper resonance within us.

OPENING OUR PSYCHIC SYSTEM

The internal practice referred to in this sutra is the practice of Kundalini Yoga—which, as we discussed in Sutra Seven, involves internalizing our energy and creating a flow inside. This vital force penetrates and opens the chakras and the sushumna as it moves up through us, dissolving the granthi and blossoming into openness. As this energy moves to the top of the head, Consciousness literally flowers. This has been described as the opening of the thousand-petaled lotus in the crown chakra. The nectar from that flowering flows down and fills the mind. You will experience this very palpably; it feels like honey is being poured over your head. The mind does not get enlightened, but it gets saturated by this nectar of Consciousness, which penetrates into it and dissolves its capacity to misunderstand.

Every element in our practice is an integral part of creating a profound spiritual transformation. Regular meditation is critical in creating the flow within. This is what opens the sushumna, allowing the very energy and vitality that created us to rise up and merge back into its own source. This is the reunion of the energy that created diversity, which created you as an individual, back into Consciousness Itself. This isn't a New Age platitude. It is an internal practice that develops the sensitive capacity of tuning in to the resonance within us. Flow is that resonance, and Presence is the field upon which it plays.

As we become immersed in and consumed by the flow, we begin to live in our center, aware of the vertical flow at all times. Then, we extend that energy into life, creating a horizontal flow out from our center, so that we are not being pulled out of ourselves, but are constantly reinvesting the energy from our engagement with life back into our psychic system. Rudi called Kundalini Yoga "psychic Drano" because by practicing it we gather enough force for the energy to rise through that system and burn away all impurity, all misunderstanding, all debris.

In a sense this is a technical process, just like learning to play a sport. There are practices to learn, and we have to remember to do them at all times. That is how we become aware; how we develop the capacity to be permanently established in the state of flow that will unfold our consciousness. The ancient Tantrics understood, experienced, and described how gathering our individuated life force and returning it back to Shiva brings enlightenment. In the process of doing that, our separate identity will dissolve. Through our meditation, we are moving back up the tattvas and remerging into Shiva, into Unity.

I cannot overemphasize to you the importance of establishing yourself in flow. My first instruction to students is, "Open your heart," but I immediately follow that with, ". . . and feel the flow." That will lead you into a state of surrender and Presence—and yet you must always bring, to the best of your ability, as much presence, stillness, and surrender to every aspect of the process itself. Opening our hearts is the beginning. It allows us to get in contact with some deeper part of ourselves. We open to the Grace that has shown up as some longing in our heart and then let it to do the work of affecting our experience.

THE TATTVAS AND THE UPAYAS

The tattvas and the upayas are essentially the reverse of each other. The tattvas elaborate on the condensation of the highest Consciousness into the density of that Consciousness—from the universal *I am*, the Source from which all life emerges, all the way down into physical matter. The tattvas demonstrate how individuality arises and then, how the mind, emotions, and physical body emerge sequentially from that platform of the separate self.

The upayas reverse this process, taking us from the state of separation back to Unity. We start with anavopaya, the path of effort, because that is what is required to move through the density in ourselves, the layers of covering we must lift off to reveal the underlying Consciousness. A person who is completely trapped in the awareness of *I am my body*, has to apply some effort to get from that level of experience to *I am*. We live under many layers of unconsciousness and misunderstanding. The density within these layers makes them almost indistinguishable from each other, so we have to use some device to break through them. This effort is our conscious meditation and disciplined practice.

As we penetrate through some density and begin to understand that *I am not just this body*, our experience of life changes. We are able to get in touch with energy, and can discern that it is the source of all form, density, and physical matter. This is shaktopaya, where we perceive that all of life is simply energy. In some translations shaktopaya is described as "the path of mind." The implication here is that shaktopaya transforms the energy that is trapped at the level of mind, and then that energy can be put into flow.

As we move up through the process of revelation, closer to tattva 1, a simpler awareness is required to have that higher experience, and this is described as shambhavopaya. There are some practices that focus solely on awareness. They advocate doing nothing but focusing on that which is already present within you. However, what is often overlooked is the work necessary for most people to get to the point where tuning directly in to Consciousness is within their capacity. That is why all the upayas play a role in spiritual development.

RECOGNITION: YOUR LIFE IS YOUR MEANS TO LIBERATION

Although we can discuss the upayas from many angles, it is important to remember that there is one principle underlying all of our sadhana: that every aspect of our own life is perfectly and Divinely offered to us as our means to liberation. Every moment and every challenge in life is an opportunity for freedom, but too often we refuse to accept what we have been given. We believe we deserve more—or that we shouldn't have to experience x, y, or z. We think our life was swapped with someone else's at birth in the hospital.

Stop insisting that this is not your life. Stop trying to change it. What is significant about our lives is not the specifics of what happens but the level of consciousness we bring into this life and the expansion of consciousness we experience as we grow. That is what we must focus on, and we do it through the path of awareness—which is the path of surrender. Let life show you its extraordinary, magnificent awareness and let go of the idea that you are the doer. That is the key to liberation. Anything else that comes up in the process, including all the "What about me?" issues, is what we surrender.

What if we were really in a state of consciously serving and consciously receiving, and yet nothing changed in life except our awareness? That would actually be the highest blessing. We all say we will surrender being the doer, but we wink and send a secret message to God, trying to negotiate for something in exchange. It is only when our outer lives don't change one bit that we have the highest possibility of understanding that we are not the doer. Piercing the veil of doership requires great subtlety of consciousness. It is a powerful membrane that will stretch forever.

Our work is to penetrate through the denser levels of understanding within us and convert them into a higher consciousness, to convert our mental and emotional struggles into flow, so that the vital force can rise up and become awareness. However, as we open to a deeper consciousness within ourselves we also become aware of the granthi. We become aware of our deepest patterns, the most incessant need to control. If we keep riding our personal merry-go-round at a particular level of density, all we are doing is putting more pressure on that density, compacting it more and more.

When an oil rigger is drilling he has one purpose in mind: striking oil. Whatever obstacle is met along the way requires the conscious choice of which tool to use. Drill bits must change as you go through the different textures of soil. Similarly, we have to assess what type of obstruction we are trying to penetrate through, and then apply various aspects of our consciousness to the densities within us.

All of our internal obstructions remain obstacles if we allow them to remain in a dense state. Whatever it takes, we have to drill and drill to release the highest Consciousness within ourselves. Then, when we open, our consciousness rises out of us like an oil geyser. Oilmen used to drill straight down, but they discovered that if the layers of earth were too thick they just couldn't get through it. So they came up with the technique of diagonal drilling, working from the side to bypass all the worst of the density. We too can reach through the density of our own limitation without going through a lot of drama with it.

The highest action is non-doing. Tune in to the Divinity that is giving life to the energy that *is* doing the work. This is an internal practice, which has nothing to do with what we accomplish in the world. The discriminating awareness needed to abide in stillness is not something we develop overnight however, which is why discipline is really important.

In my practice we have a standing joke that if we can't keep from verbally expressing our tensions, we can at least wrap some duct tape around our mouth. Similarly, we must practice binding our need to act whenever we misunderstand what is happening. Through practice, we learn to rest in stillness.

The discussion of the upayas fits beautifully into this sutra because it helps us understand which tool we need to use to penetrate whatever density we are dealing with at the moment. The discovery of and penetration through our own density is the essence of sadhana. The entire discussion of the *Pratyabhijna Hrdayam* is the recognition of the Self. We are not discovering something that suddenly manifested; we are recognizing our Divine nature, which is eternal.

Be focused on raising your consciousness by uncovering the highest in yourself, and not on the challenges that arise as you uncover that Divinity. Whatever density we have to drill through should be seen from the perspective of attaining our ultimate goal. Eleventh-century Tantric master Abhinavagupta said that with the correct longing, one could attain liberation in four forty-minute sessions. Focus on your sadhana with that degree of intensity.

चितिवह्निरवरोहपदे छन्नो ऽपि
मात्रया मेयेन्धनं प्लूष्यति

citivahniravarohapade channo 'pi
mātrayā meyendhanaṃ pluṣyati

SUTRA FOURTEEN

The fire of Consciousness—though it seems to be in a descended state—gradually burns up the fuel of the knowable.

Sutra Fourteen

The essential message of this sutra is that no state of mind can completely obscure Consciousness. Even though the dross of our mental and emotional constraints covers this eternal light, there is still some illumination filtering through. Even when we are completely unaware of our Self, Supreme Consciousness is still aware of Itself. God experiences Himself within us, although covered by the dullness of our limited state.

The good news is that, because Consciousness is never completely obscured, no matter how dense our state is, we can always find freedom. No matter how lost we are in whatever struggle we are going through—no matter how much we misunderstand and think it is about us—we can and must find within that confusion the underlying state of openness.

Mind cannot completely obscure Consciousness. It tries. It does its song and dance. Since the source of the mind is Consciousness, it can't completely cover that source, although it has a limited capacity to perceive Itself. There is always the perception of subject and object within the mind, because we can never consume objects completely. When Consciousness descends and our individuality forms, our sense of separation pervades our experience and our awareness. In that state, we can never consume "two" completely, because we are always trying to do it from the mind, which is a place of duality.

"I am" is always the supreme subject, the supreme perceiver, and from that perspective there is no possibility of *two*. However, inherent in the process of becoming an individuated expression of the whole, our immediate perception is that there's God and us. We are stuck in duality and can't see past that separation. The mind can never consume its own misunderstanding. That's the sad truth. As Einstein said, you can't solve a problem from the place it was created. We keep beating our heads against the wall, trying to prove that we can.

ATTACHMENT TO OUR MIND AND LIMITATIONS

The previous sutra described the transformation of the mind. We saw that the expansion of consciousness from the state of mind to the state of higher awareness gives us the capability of experiencing Unity. This sutra reminds us that just because our mind can become Consciousness, we must not forget that there is another force at work—namely our attachment to our mind and its limitation. Sutra fourteen is looping back, referring to the previous statement that Consciousness contracts in becoming the mind. We've encountered some powerful descriptions of the limitation of our consciousness as individuals, and the cost to us of functioning from that individuated awareness. The mind is the solidifier and the validator of that individuality, which is rooted in the perception of subject and object. The critical lesson here is that freedom does not happen in the mind.

No matter what the dross is, whether it is pain and suffering or ecstasy and celebration, it is generally determined for us by our experience of "me" and some "thing" that is happening "to me." Regardless of whether we are happy or miserable, if that experience is attached to the conditions of our life—dependent on objects that make us feel happy or sad—then we have inherently limited our capacity for freedom. We have lost sight of the place of unconditionality within us.

The mind is a thief. Even when we feel the joy of expansion and freedom, the mind will insert some subtle thought about *why* the experience has arisen. It will insinuate that there is some condition or reason for our experience, and that there is something we must do to avoid losing it. In truth, we should do nothing except surrender and let Consciousness tune us in to Itself. But understand that as soon as the mind feels any loss of control, any loss of the sense of separation, it will do its seductive dance and grab your attention some way. Don't let your mind catch you. Instead, rest in stillness, recognize the trap, and refrain from giving it energy. This is how we suspend the action of the mind and "burn the fuel of the knowable."

It is good to detach from the insistence that our mind is all-knowing. It cannot be, because it inherently separates subject and object. Just suspend that perception long enough and watch what happens. Thought has to subside into the heart, the abode of higher Consciousness. We can learn to rest there. If we do that, we don't have to work to detach from the mind, because its grip on us simply dissolves. In this way we are using our deepest consciousness to burn through the limitation of the mind—to burn through the knowable—to awaken us to what is unknowable by the mind.

When we get embroiled in some tension, we must let go of the drama long enough to ask, "Where is this coming from?" This allows us to tune deeper and deeper inside, until the grip of that binding begins to loosen. At some point we even see that the binding itself is a fabric of our imagination. Even though the situation is real in its own context, when seen from another perspective it is only an illusion that such an experience could cover our highest Consciousness.

Moving quickly through our misunderstanding creates a good deal of resistance and heat. That is the fire of Consciousness. We choose to submit ourselves to that force in order to clear out all the debris in our psychic mechanism, to allow the highest

Consciousness to be revealed within us. The alternative is to just keep spinning on our merry-go-round, and if we choose that option we will remain endlessly dizzy and confused. In our spiritual work we are trying to do more than just get over the particular drama of the moment. We are trying to free ourselves from the very place inside that needs drama and tension. That is the fast road to freedom.

This work involves the recognition of a deeper dimension of life's functioning, and tuning ourselves to the potent experience of unconditionality. Although we detach from the mind, the experience is not one of apathy. On the contrary, it is potent in its fullness. We are not spiritual ostriches, sticking our heads in the sand, rejecting or ignoring life. If any apathetic feeling arises, it may come from trying to dissociate from something without at the same time taking our awareness to a deeper place. It is from contact with that depth that we feel the potency of freedom, unconditionality, openness, and flow, and know that our true state cannot become covered by any condition.

RECOGNITION: CONSCIOUSNESS BURNS LIMITATIONS

Submitting ourselves to the fire of Consciousness means that we burn whatever comes up. We disconnect from all objects, even wonderful, blissful feelings. Why would we want to burn that? Because we don't want to get caught in the moment-by-moment enjoyment of it, but to allow immersion in the source of that bliss to become our permanent experience. This sutra is explaining that whatever end of the happy/sad pendulum we are on, if our state is based on a mental level of awareness, by definition it will include objects that are seen as separate from us. We can enjoy the beauty and diversity of the surface, but we also have to penetrate beneath that level into the source of *all* experience. We don't want the manifest level of life to limit our experience, and we only expand past this boundary by burning away all thought and emotion.

If we disconnect from their content, we learn to recognize our mind, thoughts, and emotions as simply energy in a more contracted form than our highest Consciousness. When we give thoughts and emotions strength by moving our awareness into them, we identify with the form, the object, and the content, and we become lost. We end up endlessly trying to figure out what the hell everything means, rather than understanding that all of life is energy that arises out of awareness.

The mind can't fathom this or disconnect from the subject-object relationship because the mind itself is part of the form created from energy. It is a dirty filter, a limited structure that cannot allow pure energy awareness to move through it. But what is looking at the mind? Its Source. The mind is actually the object of Consciousness—real only because there *is* something watching it. The mind won't transcend its limitations unless our own inner awareness expands and pulls the mind along with it. So we let go of trying to understand from our mind and instead live in our heart, which is seated in a place of higher Consciousness. It is our own Divine Consciousness that provides the nourishment for this to happen.

बललाभे विश्वमात्मसात्करोति

balalābhe viśvam ātmasāt karoti

SUTRA FIFTEEN

When this (the fire of Consciousness)
reaches (full) strength,
the universe becomes one's own.

Sutra Fifteen

Here is a description of how we internalize the powerful force that has created and sustained life; how we learn that it is who we are. Kundalini Yoga uses the power of inner practice to absorb this tremendous life force—pulling that energy back inside us, refining it, and making it our own. Once we have done that repeatedly, over time and with enough depth, the energy becomes our own strength, and it is from that power that we create our new experience of life.

The term in the text is *Shiva Drishti*, which means, "the assimilation of Shiva's strength." We gain that strength through the gaze of Shiva. One of the significant means Tantric practices use to attune sadhakas to this powerful Consciousness is through shaktipat. That force can be transmitted from teacher to student in four ways: by sight, touch, thought, and word. The extraordinary Grace of a shaktipat practice is that students can connect to that supreme force on an ongoing basis. Our connection to Grace through shaktipat is like recharging a car battery when it gets a little run down. We can regularly plug back in to Consciousness.

Our sadhana is to permanently establish ourselves in the flow of the vital force we contact in meditation and reinforce through shaktipat—so that we make it our own. By practicing Shiva Drishti long enough we gain the strength to dissolve our misunderstanding, our separateness, and our sense of being the doer. We not only know that we are Shiva but experience the power inherent in being That. This connection to the Divine becomes our own strength when, through the fire of Consciousness, we have opened enough to fully assimilate it. At that point the whole distinction between teacher and student dissolves. When you have your own permanent connection to the Divine, you don't need a teacher. Until then, shaktipat serves as a temporary link, a means of attuning ourselves with God. It is, at least, a recharging station.

What happens to our connection with God once we have established it? It expands further. It's like being replumbed. Our psychic mechanism is complete and full, but every once in a while God says, "Let's open it up a little more," or we ask, "Let me open this a little more." Since Consciousness is infinite, whatever subtle level of boundary we might feel within has the capacity to be dissolved. Think of the strength you can experience when you assimilate the enormous power of this manifest universe! When we pull that energy back into ourselves, it makes us bigger and better in a process of infinite evolution.

Shiva is expanding His experience of His own state all the time, and therefore we can also choose to do the same thing. That involves a lot of power, and that is exactly what this sutra is saying: When our internal fire reaches full strength, the universe becomes our own. Ironically, when we are in complete control, what do we want to do? Nothing—because we are not the doer. We simply rest in infinite stillness.

RECOGNITION: MAKING THE UNIVERSE OUR OWN

As we discussed in the previous sutra, it is by opening our hearts that we gain that strength and have access to the highest Consciousness with us. The entire power of the universe comes into us when we open our hearts. This goal is worth some investment of our time and effort. It is worth sitting in meditation long enough to find our heart—but understand that it is mostly when we are not in meditation that we have to focus on transcending duality. We can all sit in meditation and be blissful, but that experience is not real if we can't open our eyes and deal with the diversity and adversity that appear before us.

The strength needed to acquire the universe is only ours when our deepest experience is sustained with our eyes open, no matter what conditions we face. We must get out of our minds and emotions long enough to really establish ourselves in an openness that never closes. That's why Rudi used the words "work" and "test." We work to make contact with a deeper place, and we test whether we have the capacity to hold on to that depth by exposing it to the reality of our life.

We do not grow in a petri dish. Life is not a sterile environment. Every day Rudi said to us, "Open your heart, and you will be tested." The test is whether we are really serious about opening our heart and keeping it open. If you don't have that wish in you, then sit down and find it. Sit down and recognize that there is a wish trying to unfold in you, or you wouldn't even be reading a spiritual book.

Let this wish reveal itself, instead of continually trying to bury it. We don't need to change any circumstances in order to be able to find openness and a depth of consciousness in our hearts. Life is happening right now; it does not come later. We have the power and the freedom to stop concealing and start revealing. We have the power and the freedom to choose what we want in life.

चिदानन्दलाभे देहादिषु चेत्यमानेष्वपि
चिदैकात्म्यप्रतिपत्तिदार्ढ्यं जीवन्मुक्तिः

cidānandalābhe dehādiṣu cetyamāneṣv api
cidaikātmyapratipattidārḍhyaṃ jīvanmuktiḥ

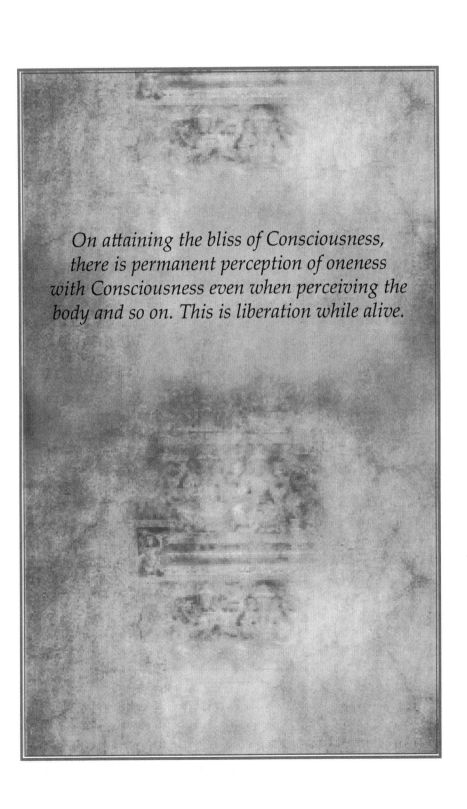

*On attaining the bliss of Consciousness,
there is permanent perception of oneness
with Consciousness even when perceiving the
body and so on. This is liberation while alive.*

Sutra Sixteen

This sutra describes the state of a liberated yogi. The highest Consciousness is available to each of us, but if your liberation is not the most important thing to you, you will not have it. If you are not prepared to surrender yourself completely, you will not live in freedom. But freedom is not found outside the context of our own lives. We can—and must—be free even while we have a body and a job. In fact, freedom is understanding and experiencing that everything in our life is an integral part of the manifestation of our own consciousness. Nothing is separate from us. This is called *jivan mukti*, freedom while alive.

Up to this point the sutras have conveyed that liberation is possible, and that attaining it is the purpose of our life. We are liberating ourselves from limited consciousness—an opportunity that is possible in every moment in our life. The primary characteristic of jivan mukti is that of being in touch with this state of Consciousness, and experiencing the peace and unconditional joy that is not affected by the day-to-day dynamics of life. Having this awareness does not negate the daily experience of life, but every moment is enjoyed from a place of freedom and nonattachment. We simply experience the Oneness of life in its perfection. This is liberation.

The unwavering experience of Oneness is a state that emerges as an expression of the bliss of Consciousness. When we can suspend all of our attachments long enough to tune in to the abiding joy in us, that immersion completely dissolves everything that makes us suffer. The good news is that we don't get to choose what we are freed from—because we all know what happens when we decide what we want and don't want to have in our lives.

OFFERING OURSELVES UNCONDITIONALLY

If we do not offer ourselves unconditionally into the fire of Consciousness, if we don't want joy more than anything else, we won't have it. If we allow *anything* to rob us of freedom, that is our choice. Attaining liberation while alive is a conscious process, requiring that we escape from being ensnared by the mind. We must consume duality in order to transcend it. This means that when we are moving through the day and our energy starts heading out toward Pluto, we reel it back. We take a breath, internalize the energy, and integrate it into the flow. Sutra Fifteen described the strength of consciousness we develop within by increasing the capacity of our psychic muscle system. We have to start where we are and use whatever level of consciousness we have to do that work. Hoping just doesn't get it done.

We must want our liberation from the place inside us that understands what liberation is, not from the part of us that doesn't understand. There is a profound yet powerful difference here. To attain liberation all of our actions must be inspired by that which is already free inside us—but how do we find it? We must penetrate through the densities of consciousness that obscure our highest awareness, and we can't do that if we are attached to the limited part of ourselves. We can't get attached to thinking, "This should not be happening to me . . . they shouldn't have done it to me . . . my spiritual life should be different than this." These types of misunderstandings create the reality of our life if we believe them.

When we push away what is actually happening to us, we avoid taking responsibility for the condition of our own experience. These thoughts are an expression of the limited part of us, a sign that our resistance to change is surfacing. When such thoughts arise, we have to keep drilling past them. On the other hand, when we get quiet enough, we can find the joy in any difficulty, and we understand how much freedom is available in letting go of everything we cling to.

DEEPER THAN MIND OR EMOTION

The beautiful thing is that as we pierce through every level of consciousness, we discover that we are no longer a prisoner of our density. When we consciously detach from our mind and emotion, we gain a sense of separation from them. We recognize them as a powerful covering, yet merely a covering.

As we penetrate through the surface form long enough to experience that whatever arises is just energy, its grip on us suddenly dissolves. We no longer give our emotions validity and we no longer give them the strength to consume our consciousness. The previous sutra stated that we have enormous power. The question is, what dimension of ourselves are we infusing with that power? We must always choose our higher will to free ourselves from our limited consciousness. Remember that it was Shiva's will to manifest, for the purpose of revealing, for the expansion of freedom. That's exactly what happens in our life if we too focus on the revealing.

When we have the understanding and awareness that life is trying to reveal its Source to us, our experience is very different. If the purpose of our life is the revealing of the highest Consciousness, all the other things we attach to (or even mistake as life's purpose) are just obscurations of that highest revelation. We may not understand this from our limited perspective, but that's the very point of spiritual practice—to uncover the place within us that *does* understand.

Any powerful experience of limitation—emotion, mind, fear, or self-rejection—is a vehicle for us to free ourselves from an invisible binding. As these limitations surface and become visible, we actually see the dross that is covering our lives. If we get caught in the struggle, drama, and pain of what arises, we reinforce that covering. But if we understand that the purpose of the experience is freedom, we can avoid getting trapped in the dynamic. We simply see it as an energy that, when buried, has kept us separate from the unwavering experience of Oneness.

THE DISSOLUTION OF SELF-ABSORPTION

Unconditional joy is the result of freeing ourselves from the most entrenched veils of duality. If liberation is what we seek, how could it be anything less than joyful to remove another layer of non-liberation? By doing that, we are fulfilling our obligation to God, our duty to reveal the highest in ourselves. But our work of loosening the grip of the ego requires the complete dissolution of all self-absorption, because experiencing individuality in that manner is the opposite of revealing the highest.

It takes as much work to sustain a state of awareness as to attain it. Sadhana doesn't stop: We don't just get enlightened and go on vacation. That kind of thinking demonstrates the inherent capacity of the veils of duality to cover back up what looks like apparent freedom. The state of jivan mukti is hard to attain. It is the complete dissolution of any separation, any difference, any thought that "I am the doer." Even a person who is deeply established within himself, will, at some point, become beguiled by one or all of those veils if they don't surrender day by day and moment by moment.

We see this in every arena. The more power we have, the greater the opportunity to get seduced by it and to think we are the doer. Even though you gathered that power by deeply trying to understand that Shiva does everything, it is still very possible to get puffed up and think you're the dude. The natural processes of contraction and expansion, of concealing and revealing, are going on all the time, and integrity requires profound surrender. Great people throughout history have had the pendulum swing from freedom back toward bondage.

Liberation while alive is a state that will develop if we focus on the joy in life instead of on everything else. Focus on the joy and celebration and understand that the conditions that come and go as the ebb and flow of life just aren't that relevant. All of them are designed to enhance that joy, even if the process of revelation hurts as it unfolds. Transformation is really only painful if we do not allow a new level of awareness to be revealed to us, if we block it by holding on to the obstacle that was exposed—the very limitation from which we need to be freed.

The process of attaining jivan mukti requires acting on all the opportunities that present themselves for our liberation. We free ourselves by surrendering everything that keeps us from Shiva. Unfortunately, we have the most powerful database within our mind that categorizes what we will and what we won't surrender. There is a reason and a justification for every form of holding on. Why not try something different? You might like it. Take all your experiences in life up to this point and trade up. Really ask, "This, or joy?" One option is distinctly different from the other.

All the mental activity necessary to function in the world has nothing to do with liberation. We can keep doing whatever we need to do to engage life. We still pay attention when we drive a car. It is simply a matter of not giving so much meaning to the things we do; not being so attached to everything that it consumes all our energy. We attach so much importance to all the stuff that goes on in our mind. We invest it with reality. Liberation has nothing to do with the mind. Rather, it has to do with freeing ourselves from the misunderstanding inherent in functioning only from the mind.

RECOGNITION: STOP STRUGGLING WITH YOUR EGO

This sutra describes the permanent experience of Oneness, and that happens after we have freed ourselves from two-ness. In other words, freedom arises after we are liberated from the grip of the ego, which is the doorkeeper to the veils of duality. To be free from the ego, we have to stop struggling with it. Stop trying to prove or disprove the validity of your ego. Stop believing that all the aspects and dynamics of your ego are real, and that you therefore must experience them on their own level in order to be free of them. So much of that activity is us just stirring the soup of duality and reinforcing concealment.

If you want to find a treasure buried three hundred feet deep in the ocean, you don't go and frolic in the waves. You just skip it. Most of us don't even get to the waves but spend our time in a little wading pool where we jump up and down and moan and groan. We use so much of our energy to reinforce the most superficial aspects of ourselves. We can fix all the problems or change our psychology. We can change our partner, or how we relate to our partner. All of that is good, but don't mistake it for freeing yourself from the grip of your ego. It is only when we loosen this grip that we get past the surface waves and get to dive deep, looking for the real treasure.

In order to expand our awareness, we have to get deeper than our mind, deeper than our understanding of what life is, by penetrating through all the surface rubble. Only then can we focus on bringing a deeper consciousness into our life. We have to spend less time working through our issues and much more time surrendering them. Just drop them. And when they come crawling back home at night, bar the door.

I cannot overemphasize that revealing the highest within us means looking for the highest and not getting caught in the things that obscure it. Instead of trying to fix and change things, we need to function from a deeper place, and we do that by opening our hearts. We tune in to the higher Consciousness that is intrinsically in our hearts and then we keep our awareness there. And every time our mind, our life, or our need to reach begins to pull us out of our center, we surrender and let it go. We spend so much time doing the opposite: closing our hearts, reaching, and demanding in a vain attempt to fill the emptiness we've just created. Spend one-hundredth of that time focusing on opening your heart, and when something difficult arises, take that energy into the fire of Consciousness and let it burn and free you.

We are talking about surrender at every level, and mostly, surrendering all the drama, tension, contraction, insecurity, and all of the reaching that comes from frolicking in the waves. Playing in the surf is fun on its own level, and if that's what you want, you've already achieved that goal. But if freeing yourself from the experience of duality is your goal, then focus on Unity, and on the source and the experience of that Oneness, instead of reinforcing the experience of duality. Focus on the joy of the extraordinary magnificence that is within you. That experience is available to you as soon as you want it.

Coming in contact with inner stillness, that state of surrender, is the prerequisite for acquiring the necessary strength to make the universe our own—to control whether or not we are bound by our ego. This is the point of meditation, of tuning in, finding a bigger resonance inside, and letting it reveal itself. We dive deep and make contact with it. As we bring this resonance out into our daily lives it will have an effect on our capacity to really let go. Sometimes we may lose contact with what we found within. That's fine; we just start over again.

मध्यविकासाच्चिदानन्दलाभः

madhyavikāsāc cidānandalābhaḥ

SUTRA SEVENTEEN

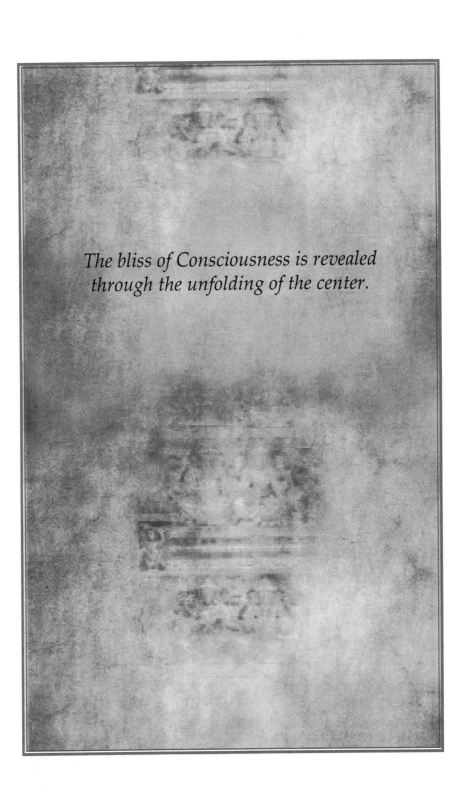

The bliss of Consciousness is revealed through the unfolding of the center.

Sutra Seventeen

Here we have an emphatic statement that unconditional joy is the result of opening our hearts. There are no conditions necessary and nothing in our lives we have to change in order to do that—but by opening our hearts and living from that center, our relationship to all conditions profoundly changes. Opening our hearts is the act of receiving Grace, the Divine force of revealing. It is closing our hearts that perpetuates concealing.

There are three loci of heart within us: our heart chakra, the center of the head, and the crown—what Nityananda called the "heart-space"—and we must open them all. My first instruction to students is to "open your heart," because that this is where we can tune in to God and feel the resonance of the highest Self within us. Our longing for realization emerges from the heart. The longing begins as a whisper from within, and we nourish it and fulfill its purpose by transforming that whisper into our own conscious wish. This first touch of Grace gives us the capacity to move out of concealment, to consciously tune in, open our hearts, and feel God.

If we did nothing else for the rest of our lives except tune in and open our hearts, we would find our freedom. It is that powerful and that simple. All of our meditation techniques, including the double-breath, are designed to take the energy of our life and of our awareness and tune it back to its Source. We start to recognize that all of life came from the center of God's heart, which we first experience as our heart. Even in

217

the beginning, when we may not clearly experience our heart chakra—and the profound Grace of longing seems to come out of nowhere—what we feel is still our own heart starting to open.

Too often, instead of opening our hearts, we run around like hamsters on a spinning wheel, constantly in motion, creating all the drama in our life. We think we have to do that to generate and control this silly life we are living, not noticing how expansive and huge it actually is. Running on the wheel generates the silt of impurities that gets deposited in our psychic mechanism. This is what buries our awareness, and the result is that only a trickle of light, a whisper of longing, filters through to wake us up.

There is only one solution: Stop running in circles. Get off the wheel that goes nowhere. Freedom will only unfold after we have stopped living in the tension of life and begin to live in our heart. We have spent lifetimes doing the opposite, and that is why we must feed our wish by consciously opening, again and again. If you are with me on my deathbed, the last thing I will say to you will still be, "open your heart." Why wait until you are on *your* deathbed to realize that you have been on the same wheel, repeating the same patterns, lifetime after lifetime?

KUNDALINI CLEARS THE SUSHUMNA

The Kundalini energy in us has been buried under lifetimes of debris. It has been smothered to the point that it can't breathe and can't flow. That is why Kundalini is described as being dormant in the base of the spine. So we take a breath into our heart and find a little space, a small channel in which to draw the energy down to the base of the spine. From there it rises back up, penetrating through the debris, opening every chakra and dissolving the bigger knots of the granthi. This is how we cultivate a consistent inner flow of energy within us, a circuit that unites the descending force moving down the front with the ascending force coming up the back from the base of the spine.

We've discussed that the structure of the individual has four bodies. Three of them travel with the transmigratory soul: the causal body (which is the conscious body), the energetic or pranic body, and the subtle body (our psychic system). The physical body does not move from life to life; it just gets draped over the other three as we incarnate. But all of our baggage travels with us—all of the accumulated tension and karma of lifetimes is there in our sushumna. The essence of Kundalini Yoga, and any Tantric practice, is the opening of the sushumna, and that is the result of freeing ourselves of all the impurities lodged there.

It is the rising of our life force, penetrating and clearing the chakras and the granthi as it moves back to the center of the head, which clears the sushumna and allows us to be fully established in our center. By opening our hearts, by freeing the vital energy to flow through and open in our sushumna, our individuated life force merges with God. Our experience of oneness with God unfolds in the heart-space.

The chakras are like train stations on the sushumna, which is the railway that leads to the heart-space. We must make sure the tracks are clean because any debris along the way can derail the journey. Our liberation is found in the last station, but it also happens all the way along the rail. If we don't free ourselves station by station, if we don't create a pure track for our life force to flow on, something will catch our awareness and pull us off the track. We have to ride the train all the way to freedom, and while some of the stations along the way might be quite attractive, the treasure is only available at the final destination.

MERGING WITH GOD

It is in our heart chakra that we begin to feel God, but it is in the heart-space that we merge with God. It is where we free ourselves from our separate identity and live in jivan mukti, the unwavering experience of oneness with our Divine Source. We still have a body. We still function in the world, but now God is living *as* us. Jivan mukti is experienced in this lifetime—not after we die. That level of realization is described in many ways, in every tradition, but the reality is ours only when we live it. The sadhana is getting to center, staying in center, and becoming that center.

Our life is a preparation for merging back into Shiva. In the process, we are freed from all misunderstanding and from the grip of the ego. Once that happens, the veils of duality are dissolved and we recognize ourselves as an expression of the Divine. As our heart begins to open we may see diversity, but we move past the duality in that diversity. "Love thy neighbor as thyself" is not just a nice slogan. It is a description of the reality of experiencing everything as oneself.

This is the progression of our spiritual work, and it all happens in Shiva's heart. Your life is not about you, unless you stay on the little hamster wheel. The practice of Kundalini Yoga, the raising of the energy within the psychic channels and the awakening of Consciousness, is what transforms us. It takes us from our wish—that initial opening of the heart—to feeling God in some way, and eventually to feeling something deeper and deeper in ourselves until we finally merge with the source of that feeling.

Freeing ourselves of the impurities of misunderstanding brings us to the recognition of the Self. Remember that *Pratyabhijna Hrdayam* means *"the heart of recognition."* We're able to recognize our own Self when we open our heart, feel the flow, free the sushumna of all the lifetimes of debris, feel the stillness in the center of the head, and surrender into the Divine. These are the practices that lead to the recognition that there is only One Heart—God's.

In its essence, this is not a different description or discussion than that of the upayas. The effort of anavopaya is to open our heart. The path of shaktopaya is to live in flow and to allow that flow to free us of all impurities. The work of shambhavopaya is to live in Divine Presence, to be in the state of surrender in the heart-space. All of these means require some focus and they all involve opening our heart, keeping it open, and allowing that to free us. There is no challenge, no pain, and no difficulty that we cannot free ourselves of by opening our hearts. The bigger the challenge or pain, the bigger we have to open. That is, in fact, the purpose of coming face to face with difficulties—they give us the opportunity to open and to consume our misunderstanding.

THE UNFOLDING OF OUR CENTER

The heart can open infinitely and it has to, because the capacity to create misunderstanding within ourselves is also infinite. True joy and fulfillment arise when we permanently open our center. This sutra is wonderful because it says that the bliss of Consciousness is revealed through the *unfolding* of our center, not the creation of it. If you find that your center is contracted, even to the point that you can barely feel it, start expanding it. You can't take a sledgehammer and break open your heart from the outside. It may feel like concrete, but the space within it that needs to be expanded can only be accessed from the inside.

Every once in a while, a few angels may come into our lives and use that sledgehammer. Angels don't come with fairy dust— they come armed with enough force to crack open our hearts. Be grateful for these angels, even though on the surface they may look like devils. Beauty is in the eye of the beholder. We hear stories about Jesus coming to someone's door only to find people rejecting Him because they thought He was a beggar.

We must reach into our hearts and find the joy. Experience the Grace of being alive and conscious and expand that. Grow your joy. Why grow anything else? Everything that happens on the surface of our life is the outcome of living in the veils of duality. Focusing on that level only takes us further away from our center. It only builds up more layers of misunderstanding to cloud our perception. So we use our awareness to penetrate through all that, to find our center and then expand it.

We cannot find our center by looking with the mind. Nor can we imagine it, because imagination is from the mind. We must find our openness, center, and flow by feeling it, by refining and focusing our awareness and tuning in to that internal resonance.

The mind can't do that; it can only remind us that we need to use a finer instrument to tune inside. The mind normally does the opposite; it projects outward. So we can only reverse that direction by using a subtler mechanism. Only then does the mind, which is condensed Consciousness, return to its expanded state.

Whether we are in meditation or in daily activity, if we keep trying to engage in life from our mind, we will stay on the surface. Rudi said that "the mind is the slayer of the soul" because if we can't make contact with ourselves, the soul might as well be dead; it is not part of our life. If we want to change that pattern, if we want to learn to really feel inside, we start by tuning in to our heart. Then we take some of the energy from the dynamics of the day and pull that inside to further nourish the heart and the psychic body. This is what creates the muscles that have the capacity to feel deeper.

The payment for our liberation is the conscious absorption of all life force back into its source. Our psychic body is the vehicle that we have been given for this assimilation. We engage in a conscious process of becoming permanently established in the inner flow, and taking all our individuality back into our sushumna and up into the heart-space. This is the refining process that turns all denser, grosser, thicker energy into pure energy and light, which can then rise up and meet Pure Consciousness.

That is the awakening of the Kundalini. It is the experience of merging with God and recognizing that we *are* that Divinity.

RECOGNITION: CHOOSING TO STAY IN OUR CENTER

The Grace of our lives is what enables us to get off of our hamster wheel and look for the omnipresent, unconditional joy that is always available to us. Instead of looking for love in all the wrong places, look for the source of all love. It is only on this basis that our experience of loving someone else will be a celebration of fulfillment rather than an expression of need.

We can love our own life the same way, and we should do so because we already have it. There are no trade-ins in this life. Opening our hearts means finding the joy and perfection in every moment. In the heart, there is no thought, no emotion, no limited understanding, no contraction, no pattern, and no veils of duality.

We can envision all of life lying in concentric circles revolving around one central Source. As we move outward from there, we find the veils of duality and then the grip of the ego. In that egoic level are all the attachments, resistance, tensions, thought-construct, biological imperatives, perceptions, contractions, projections, emotions, desires, and the need to control. The bad news is that this list could go on indefinitely. The good news is that we have the power to choose where we center ourselves. If we are centered in any of the limitations of the ego, our life and universe emanate from there.

Our center can be anywhere, but the center of liberation is God's heart, which is, of course, within our own heart-space. To find God's center, we begin in our heart chakra. That will lead us to the center of the sushumna, to the center of the head, and finally, to the center of the heart-space, the place Nityananda also described as the "sky of Consciousness."

We are making the universe our own. And although we can do anything we want with that strength, when we attain it, the only thing we really want to do is allow it to take us further into God. We know we're on the right track when we feel the bliss of Consciousness, but we have to find joy even in the most contracted experience. It's the same joy, because, in truth, there is only Unity.

विकल्पक्षयशक्तिसंकोचविकास-
वाहच्छेदाद्यन्तकोटिनिभालनादय इहोपायाः

vikalpakṣayaśaktisaṃkocavikāsa-
vāhacchedādyantakoṭinibhālanādaya ihopāyāḥ

SUTRA EIGHTEEN

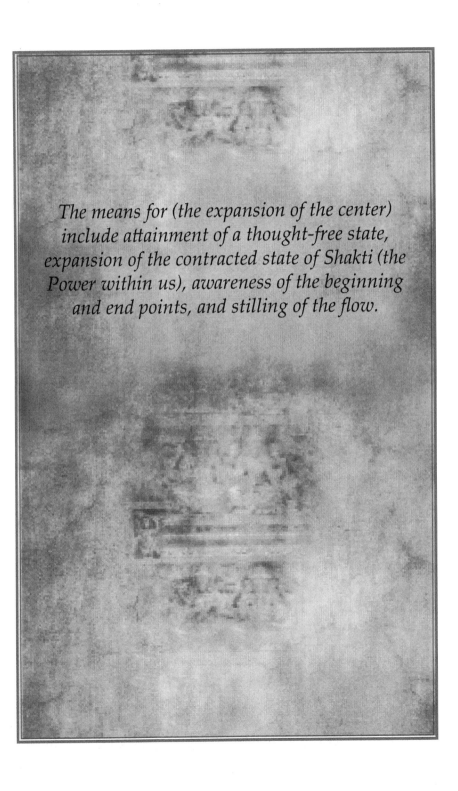

The means for (the expansion of the center) include attainment of a thought-free state, expansion of the contracted state of Shakti (the Power within us), awareness of the beginning and end points, and stilling of the flow.

Sutra Eighteen

Sutra Seventeen said that the bliss of Consciousness is attained through the unfoldment of the center, and here we have a fuller discussion of how that expansion develops. We see that the methods of opening our center include a thought-free state, and it's important to note that this is the *dissolution* of thoughts—not understanding, analyzing, or watching them. The Sanskrit term *nirvikalpa samadhi* clearly tells us that this is a thought-free state of samadhi.

The first thing we have to do to dissolve our thoughts is detach from them. Recognize that our thoughts are the effect of our limited perspective and understanding. As we've discussed, thoughts come from the mind. They are what the mind does to validate itself, and then we attach ourselves to those thoughts to further reinforce our beliefs and perceptions. But how do we reverse that attachment?

Consciousness Itself has no thought because It has no object to attach Itself to. In earlier sutras, Kshemaraja told us that although mind is a contraction of Consciousness, it can expand back into Consciousness. This is a clue that should help us understand that we need to expand beyond thought, mind, and perception in order to be free from our attachment to them. As Sutra Seventeen explained, this expansion happens in our center, through the opening of our heart. This is how we learn to live in the bliss of Consciousness.

A thought-free state is not the equivalent of having a spiritual lobotomy. Our intellect serves a purpose, which is to think and interact with the world. We do not cease paying attention to whatever tasks are at hand, but this is very different from engaging in the mental projections that come from our attachments and from our limited perspective. It's important to really understand this difference because otherwise we might fear that if we open our hearts and become conscious, we will stop being functional. This is silly! The reality is that we are functioning human beings *because* we have a center and are conscious.

OVERCOMING FEAR

We may be afraid of many things, but fear itself does not have much validity. Fear is a projection from within ourself to protect something. It attaches to our thoughts so that it can plant a bigger hook in us, but fear itself has nothing to do with our thoughts. The real source of fear is our ego. The ego is afraid of its own dissolution, because it has no substance. It never existed as the separate entity it proclaims itself to be. Spiritual work deeply threatens the ego, and that is something we all must face. If we get caught up in worry about how much money is in our bank account, we miss the opportunity to penetrate underneath that and see what is really binding us—and that is living in duality.

Thoughts are like blades of grass; there are millions of them and they are inconsequential. We can spend an infinite amount of time with our thoughts yet never get free of their grip. It is only when we open our hearts that we are not caught up in the mind and ego. Part of opening our hearts is being willing to face the source of our fear. We cannot get past the constant noise in our minds if we are not willing to detach from the fear that underlies our thinking. There is no safety net in spiritual work. That's why we can feel both the freedom and the scariness of doing it.

Until we get past our mental constructs, we cannot approach stillness or be centered in our hearts. The cessation of thought is a critical part of tuning in to the Consciousness that created the mind—that created the thought itself. But too often we can't let go of whatever it is that hooks us because we are attached to it, and because we created our identity through it. Of course there is going to be some fear when our identity is challenged. But how well has holding on to your identity worked out for you? End of discussion. If we all lived in the bliss we attained through the expansion of the center, we wouldn't need to discuss our attachment to the mind.

Let's face it: We are unwilling to let go of the things we say we don't want. Instead, we actively choose to hold on to them, because that reinforces our separateness. If we want freedom, we must leap off the precipice of our identity. We cannot dissolve the veils of duality any other way. It is black and white. There is no gray area. We can't get to the precipice and jump halfway off. Instead of being afraid of that moment of surrender, be very afraid that you may not even get there. As Rudi said, "Heaven is living with God, and hell is having to live with yourself."

THOUGHTS SUSTAIN OUR IDENTITY

We have discussed how our thoughts are the circus that creates and sustains our identity. They are what keep us focused outward, away from our Self—even though we believe that our thoughts are about us. We are constantly projecting about somebody else, or ourselves in relation to somebody else, or one thing or another. Thoughts have a perpetual theme, which is, "What's going to happen to me?" That mantra of stupidity is repeated five million time a day, no matter what we are doing. This preoccupation maintains our limited identity, and so we must dissolve our thoughts in order to really face our true Self.

We have about sixty thousand thoughts a day. Spanda philosophy describes how one thought gives rise to a second, which creates a third, and so on, ad infinitum. We've seen that the technique for counteracting this ongoing process is to be still and watch a thought arise, but give it no content. Recognize that the potential content comes from our mind, which is trying to distract us from our Self. The entire Spanda theory is based on the canon that thought-construct is the bondage of life. This is a powerful statement. Equally important is the understanding that we can be free of thought-construct.

The cessation of thought happens when we tune our awareness in to our heart, in to a deeper, higher, more expanded consciousness. But our identity is threatened every time we experience a consciousness that is bigger than the separateness. Because our ego wants to maintain the status quo, we must learn to pay attention in order to prevent our habitual patterns from continuing. These patterns repeat themselves because we keep giving them life. We attach to them and give them validity.

Even though we may understand theoretically that we can avoid giving form to our thoughts, tensions, contractions, and patterns, it takes some time to learn how to pull our energy back inside and not let the form arise. In time, we shorten the length of the cycle of the creation, maintenance, and dissolution of our patterns. The duration of our thoughts shrinks as we recognize that they are just arising, doing their dance, and subsiding.

We are what we love. If we love our thoughts, we are our thoughts. We have to get over ourselves and stop fighting to defend our identity. We have to trust that God has something more in store for us than the life we think we are living. Why should we care if we lose that? God is living as us and He is infinite and everpresent. There is no end to our lives, but there is an end to all the things we think we need in this life. Once we have jumped from the precipice, we realize that we don't need everything we thought we must have.

FUNCTIONING FROM A DIFFERENT PLACE

It is amazing to see the intense attachment we have to our misunderstanding. It's like the seven blind men trying to understand the elephant: They will never get it right. Our mind will never get it right. Why do we try to convince ourselves, over and over again, that our mind and thoughts are so real and important? In order to attain the cessation of our thoughts we have to want to let go of them. Meditating without fully letting go does not bring the kind of depth and sincerity necessary to really free ourselves from the limited perspective of the ego. I've said that your life is not about you . . . but your thoughts *are* about you because even if their topic is someone else, it is always in relationship to you.

The previous sutra explained that we experience bliss when we rest in our center. It is thoughts of "what's going to happen to me" that really pull us out of our Self. So when a thought threatens to catch us, we have to dissolve it by taking a breath and pulling that energy back inside. We bypass the content and simply put the energy that gave life to the thought back into the flow and channel it into a deeper part of us.

When we really understand this principle, life changes because we can function from a different place, centered in our deepest Self. We are truly present in every moment, accepting the life God has given us. Our mind arises and functions from the misunderstanding that we are incomplete—and thoughts are the dance of the mind. It is only our thoughts that look back and feel regret, or project forward and fear the future. Thoughts then reinforce our experience that we are not complete in this very moment.

What do you want in this life? Do you want to continually reinforce your separation from God, or do you want to live in union? If I were you, I would be really afraid that union *won't* take place. I would let *that* fear drive me crazy, because without a profound depth of longing we will not get to the edge of our identity. And if we maintain our thoughts, we cannot even get close to the precipice. Spiritual growth is an organic process of unfolding, and we each have to do that unfolding for ourselves. Don't misunderstand: It will get scarier than all the horror movies in the world. We fear the precipice, but don't really have a clue about what we will face in the moment of ultimate surrender. However, the fear should not be in letting go; what we *should* fear is that we will not let go.

To get through that transformation, we have to find the joy in whatever level of freedom is unfolding at every moment. If we do this, there is no fear and no thought of what comes next. The joy builds until it is so much bigger than the fear that by the time we get to the ultimate point of spiritual practice—the dissolving of our separate identity—we can simply let go, as if our joy was exhaling.

Fear boils down to one thing: our struggle with ourselves and with our lives. These are really not separate issues since our lives are a reflection of our inner state. The antidote to fear is to focus on the joy of unfolding and to surrender our misunderstanding. Focus on knowing that our life is God unfolding as us, for the simple purpose of seeking Joy, with a capital J. True joy is beyond any conception of "happiness," which is based on some condition in our lives that pleases us for a short while. If we simply accept our life in its perfection, as it is right now, we would move beyond conditional happiness. We would cease fighting about giving up our thoughts. We would stop defending our limitations, because all of that is irrelevant in the face of unconditional joy.

EXPANSION OF THE CONTRACTED STATE OF SHAKTI (THE POWER WITHIN US)

Like the natural rhythm of breathing, the rising and subsiding of life happens on the field of Consciousness. The means for opening our center is to be aware of both the expansion and contraction of one's power, but we tend to focus on and desire only expansion. We are disturbed when contraction happens instead of understanding it as part of the pulsation of Consciousness.

If we watch any expansion and contraction, on whatever level we are dealing with, we recognize its source is our center. It's not really relevant to distinguish between contraction and expansion; the important point is how that pulsation serves to bring our consciousness into center. We can get caught in either the fear of losing our power or in the single focus of expanding it. Our center gets bigger by living in the pulsation of energy, being present with it, watching it, and understanding that it is the natural arising and subsiding of the life that emerged from the simple expression of Consciousness.

You can't be particularly attached to any expansion because at some point it will contract. That is the inherent nature of pulsation. Our lives arise and subside in Shiva. The question is always, can we find our center and allow it to get bigger? We've seen that the bliss of Consciousness is attained through the expansion of center. All of life functions from there. It's amazing that scientists keep finding essence inside of essence. The ancient Tantrics were inner scientists whose only instrument of measurement was their own consciousness. They recognized that experiences can either pull us out of ourselves—when the mind projects into the future or dwells upon the past—or allow us to penetrate deeper into our center.

The details of the expansion and contraction are just the play of Shiva. The deeper issue is whether that pulsation is revealing or concealing our life as the center of that Consciousness. If we are busy concealing we are not allowing revealing to take place. The problem is our unwillingness to get still and centered enough in our hearts to let revelation show itself. That's why we must remember to focus on staying centered, not on what happens along the way.

235

All power ultimately belongs to Shiva, and we have examined how we attain that power of Consciousness. Now it is ours to do with as we want, but if we use power to penetrate into our center we are using it for its intended purpose. Your life was given to you for your freedom; it is being lived as you for Shiva's freedom. Without ever losing Himself, Shiva expands and contracts — and through that process His freedom enjoys infinite expansion.

It's only when we think we are doing the expanding and contracting that we believe we are the agent, become attached to the process, and think we have some control over it. Through our spiritual discipline, as our inner vibration expands and contracts, it naturally gets bigger. That's the process. Why would we be afraid of life getting bigger? Our power expands to the extent that we recognize that it is not really ours but Shiva's. All that happens unfolds back on itself from within Him.

AWARENESS OF THE BEGINNING AND END POINTS

Being aware of the beginning and end points means being aware of the center, and, most importantly, being established in stillness and Presence. This inner space is accessed and expressed in a number of ways — specifically in our breath, the pulsation of our heart, and in the field of action. We can be aware of the beginning and end points in each of these key areas because we observe them from our center.

The first thing we must therefore do is find the center. In my practice and teaching we use the double-breath to tune our energy back inside, which directs our awareness inward. This is the essence of the progression I've described as breath, chakra, flow, and Presence. We start by bringing such discrimination to the awareness of our breath that we are able to focus on the center from which the breath emerges. We can then watch the pulsation of breath as it extends from that center, reaches its apex, and subsides back to its source. Finally, we let go into that stillpoint, which further expands the inner dimensions of our awareness, extending the scope of our center beyond the body.

Because every experience arises and subsides on our own field of consciousness, we can rest in the stillpoint and stay centered in a state of openness as we engage in the activities of life. This is how we develop the ability to see through our limited perspective. We can also view our thoughts as the arising and subsiding of the energy, or "action," of the mind.

When we do not attach our awareness to thoughts and thereby give them form, but simply allow them to begin and end, we discover a powerful means of freeing ourselves from the grip of the ego. Each time a limiting thought is created by the mind we can remain in stillness; whatever unfolds does not necessitate an action or reaction.

Stillness is the door into Presence, and contacting stillness in the awareness of the beginning and end points is how we develop the ability to permanently live in that state. Stillness is found between any two points—be it in our breath, thought, action, emotion, physical movement, sound, or experience. Within any "two" is the entry point into the Oneness of Consciousness.

STILLING OF THE FLOW

Through repeatedly focusing on the breath we become more and more aware of the pulsation of Consciousness from the center, which is our own heart. As we advance in our practice we can follow the arising and subsiding, the beginning and end of that pulsating consciousness without engaging the breath. This pulsation is the breath inside the breath—the internal breath—which is not dependent on any inflow or outflow of the gross breath.

We think we have to breathe to be alive, but that level of breath is really a superficial effect of the internal breath. There are many accounts of saints who could exist in a state of suspension of breath — and it happens because they are attuned to the inner breath. It is only their physical body that stops breathing.

The fact that we don't even have to breathe to be alive should be a very pointed reminder that our life is not about us. We are alive because we are being breathed by God. Think about how much power we would feel if we could simply tune in to the internal breath, the breath of God.

The stilling of the flow of the incoming and outgoing vital energy also happens in the stillpoint in our center. That connection would completely transform any attachment to our thoughts — because a very basic assumption was proven wrong by the discovery that even our vital force does not go in and out as we believed it did.

RECOGNITION: SUBTLE DISCRIMINATION

This sutra provides a perfect definition of "subtle discrimination," which is the term Nityananda used to describe how we penetrate past the surface of life. He said that we must learn to see the subtle in the gross, the One in the many. It is vital for us to recognize that we will not find that sensitivity and awareness without profound, deep, disciplined inner work.

This degree of internal focus is what is needed if we wish to transform our consciousness and our experience of life. Understanding the subtle forces within, and freeing ourselves of all patterns, contractions, and tensions, is a conscious process that only develops as an expression of a deep longing and a life dedicated to true spiritual freedom.

The next sutra will further elaborate the understanding that the only way to experience this discriminating subtlety is to internalize our life force, and that does not just happen while we are sitting on our cushion in formal meditation. Anyone can sit and meditate for a period of time and be able to tune in, get their thoughts under control, and feel blissful. We must, of course, do that, but our disciplined internal practice has to continue when our eyes are open, when we face the appearance of duality. That is how we discover that there is no internal or external; there is only one field of Consciousness.

समाधिसंस्कारवति व्युत्थाने भूयो
भूयश्चिदैक्यामर्शान्नित्योदितसमाधिलाभः

samādhisaṃskāravati vyutthāne
bhūyo bhūyaś cidaikyāmarśān
nityoditasamādhilābhaḥ

SUTRA NINETEEN

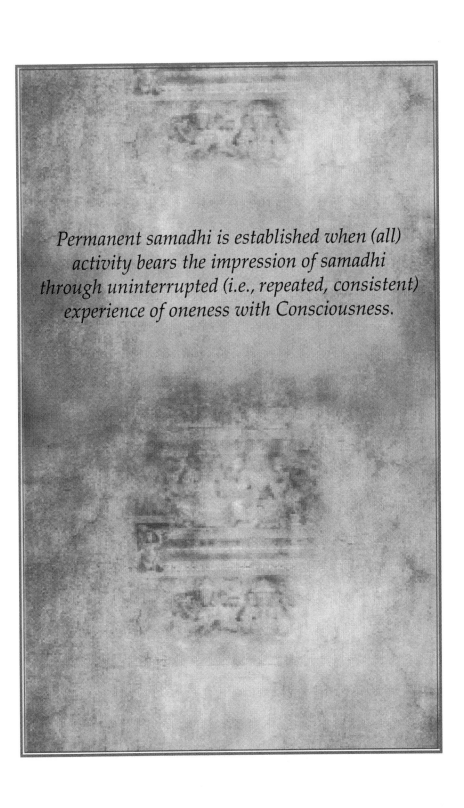

*Permanent samadhi is established when (all)
activity bears the impression of samadhi
through uninterrupted (i.e., repeated, consistent)
experience of oneness with Consciousness.*

Sutra Nineteen

We have discussed the importance of meditation, of finding our capacity for subtle discrimination, and that whatever depth we discover within us must be expressed as we open our eyes. That is what makes it real. When we repeatedly attune to the resonance of God in ourselves, we are absorbed back into our Source. As we immerse ourselves in Consciousness and allow it to fully reveal Itself, we start to penetrate through duality.

We all have had the experience of sitting in meditation and becoming less and less aware of our thoughts, distractions, pain, and suffering—and increasingly more in tune with joy and openness. This is the point of meditation, whatever form it takes. This sutra instructs us to meditate, to contact samadhi, and then, when we get up off our cushion, to repeatedly stay in contact with our experience. This is how we carry our meditation experience into our life.

In order to fully integrate what we at first believe to be our "inner" versus our "outer" experience, we must engage in a number of aspects of whatever spiritual practice we have chosen. These facets of our sadhana work as a matrix of approaches to bring the impression of samadhi out into our lives. In the following paragraphs I'll briefly delineate some of the most important of these practices and explain how they apply to the growth of consciousness that we've been discussing throughout the sutras.

SURRENDER IS THE FOUNDATION OF ALL PRACTICE

All facets of sadhana—disciplined inner practice, conscious choice, service, and engagement with a teacher—must happen on the field of surrender. That is how we repeatedly contact our highest Consciousness. We must surrender all that keeps us from Shiva. Let go of the idea that you will surrender only under certain conditions. Remember that surrender is both a practice and a state that is the result of practice. It is the practice of finding a deeper surrender, and ultimately dissolving our will unconditionally into God's will.

Surrender is what we *do* until eventually it matures into a state we live from. No matter what level of practice, and whether we have been doing our sadhana for one day or fifty years, if we forget to surrender, we will lose our way. Grace is trying to free us, to reveal our Self, and we have to accept that this happens on God's terms, not ours. Who are we to debate with Grace about how our freedom should take place? Every moment of our lives, God is trying to expose our misunderstanding, but so much of the time we just dig in our heels and insist that we know better. Living in surrender is how we allow God to show us our life.

A ROOM WITH A DIFFERENT VIEW

We have to be aware *from* Consciousness, instead of from an ego that inherently sees the world only in terms of diversity. We control where we focus our consciousness and have the ability to know when we are moving out of our center—and then we can reverse the process by choosing revelation instead of remaining in the grip of concealment. This is how we make unity with Consciousness constant in our lives.

Our inner state is both a filter of how we perceive things and of how our life expresses itself. If, for example, fear is our filter, we understand and perceive everything we encounter in terms of that emotion. We then express and reach out from that state instead of from a state of joy and openness. Through our meditation, by focusing on our highest Self, we begin to feel our true essence—and that becomes the energy and awareness we can consciously maintain as we engage with the world. We develop the ability to sustain an uninterrupted experience of oneness with Consciousness by extending ourselves again and again into what we mistakenly perceive as duality.

So look out from the inner window. Let the light of your own Consciousness illuminate what you are seeing. Learn to see the One in the many. As we try to live from our center, the world becomes our testing lab. It is where we mark our progress in the quest to make the highest Consciousness permanently ours. Every time we engage in some dynamic we don't understand, instead of getting lost in it, we learn to tune back to our Self. By doing this we come to recognize that all lack of clarity is based on a misunderstanding within us. It has nothing to do with the object, the situation, or with any conditions. Tuning in to higher Consciousness requires cleaning our filter of perception by dissolving all the internal debris, until there is nothing left to obscure Unity.

DISCIPLINED INNER PRACTICE

Our sadhana is contemplating our identity with Consciousness again and again in the state of meditation and then extending that into life. When we want to develop this capacity to grow spiritually, a disciplined inner practice is critical. We need to go to the gym every day to build a muscle system. Sometimes we want to go and sometimes we do not, but we know that if building powerful muscles is important to us, we must have the discipline to do the work. The same principle applies to spiritual practice. We create an inner discipline so that when our resistance comes up, we fall back on the strength and attachment to our wish, and we practice even when we do not want to.

In some ways, as we go deeper, the resistance gets worse because a deeper part of us is now facing its own dissolution. Growing spiritually is the hardest thing one can ever do in life. But if we seek that treasure, then we hold on to our wish and our commitment no matter how difficult it is or how long it takes. We have to find a place in us that does not struggle with the process. We must be willing to repeatedly throw ourselves into the fire of Consciousness until our limited awareness is transformed into Divine awareness. This is a radical change that requires a deep level of commitment and surrender. It requires more than a brief feeling of resolve or an idealistic vision. We must be committed to working, to really feeling a change inside of us.

It will take some time of regular practice before we are able to effect that change, so the resolve is to keep reaching inside. The shift in our consciousness comes from finding that deeper place again and again. There is only one true resolve—to become free by living in a state that is not dependent on any condition. Be dedicated to living in the heart of God, and recognize that whatever we do should be in service to that intention.

This commitment is our primary reply to Grace, to the force of revelation that mysteriously showed up, even if we weren't looking or asking for it, and even if we at first tried to reject it. When Grace begins to reveal our highest Self, the only response can be love, gratitude, and devotion—which must be expressed as a practice that has no inner or outer dimension.

THE CONSCIOUS CHOICE TO LOVE OUR LIVES

An important aspect of sadhana is conscious choice, and the highest choice we can make in any moment is to recognize our freedom instead of identifying with our bondage. In order to have an uninterrupted experience of oneness with Consciousness, we must not allow the perception of duality to distract us and cover up our highest Self.

We ourselves have created the very life that has confused us; the choice is to tune past that, to find the Source that underlies it all. Consciousness has this capacity to be aware of Itself and that is the level of discrimination we must bring to our sadhana, moment by moment. The ability to penetrate through the arising and subsiding, to experience that everything is happening on the field of Consciousness, is the definition of revelation.

The experience of simplicity, joy, and effulgence that we find in our hearts when we meditate should also be found in our engagement with daily life. Normally our experience is close to the opposite, so we have to consciously embody and extend from openness if we wish to transform how we live. When we do that we cease rejecting and trying to change life, and instead, simply love what is. By living the life God gave us instead of the one we are always trying to fabricate, we demonstrate our devotion to life and our gratefulness to That which gave it to us.

We have an amazing capacity to romanticize, fantasize, and believe our life is somewhere else. Our life is here, right now, every single day. Are we going to live in the drama and suffering we create or in the simplicity and unconditional joy available to us? When we constantly choose to focus on an imaginary "better" life, we deny ourselves the recognition of how incredible life is, as it is.

Love, gratitude, and devotion are the emergent qualities of surrender, but they often get squeezed out by the steel vice of our ego. An initial state of openness is often compressed until there is nothing left of the expansion. When that happens, we have to close our eyes, tune in, and find ourselves again. Then, as soon as we rediscover the place of openness and clarity inside, how could we wish to do anything else but to express that as we reengage life? But it takes repeatedly reopening to develop the capacity to remain open, no matter what we encounter in our day.

RELATIONSHIP WITH A TEACHER AND SHAKTIPAT

The open-eyes shaktipat transmission class that is an integral part of my practice is a powerful way of contacting and integrating Divine energy and awareness. The energy of shaktipat is the flow of Grace that can cut through any level of density within us, greatly augmenting whatever inner work we do on our own. That Divine nourishment feeds the Divinity within, allowing it to emerge and reveal itself to us. Shaktipat is love freely given, a living spiritual force that opens the door within us and provides the nourishment and support necessary to keep that door open.

During shaktipat, the teacher is essentially a tuning fork that enables the student's psychic mechanism to resonate with a higher force. Through engagement with a teacher, the student comes in contact with the energy field that is the Grace of that lineage. Shaktipat may be offered in a formal class, but we can tune in and identify with that Consciousness again and again, regardless of our physical proximity to the teacher. Grace is available all the time, to take when we want it.

If we don't break down the deep levels of resistance within us, we will never get to reach into and access the Self. The connection to the vital force of the teacher is critical in breaking down our resistance. We are using the teacher to fan the flames of our own fire. It is only when we no longer need this energy that we no longer need a teacher. A teacher is part of the Grace of our lives, of our own Divinity trying to free us.

SEVA AND FREEING OURSELVES FROM KARMA

Seva, or selfless service, is the natural expression of openness and surrender. It comes from establishing one's identity in Consciousness. The unwillingness to serve is the result of not being identified with our own highest Consciousness, but the opposite is also true. When we contact our inner depth, we can't wait for the next opportunity to give.

Service is the heartfelt response to being in contact with our highest Self, and that includes both selflessly serving and selflessly receiving. We are living in God's will, serving the Divine within us. There is no higher ecstasy than to live in God's service because that is when we recognize that we are the vehicle through which God functions in the world. We experience that God is living as us. It has been said that God's favorite name for Himself is "the servant of servants." Those words perfectly express the beauty of that state.

Service is also how we free ourselves from karma. Karma is not what happens to us; it arises from our actions in response to what happens. Karma is also an expression of the energy of willfulness that we most often function from in our lives, and it is therefore through engagement with the world that we can free ourselves from our karma. We created karma in that realm, and we have to dissolve it in that same level of consciousness. This doesn't mean we have to act on every karmic situation that comes back around, but we do have to be conscious enough to recognize it as a repeating pattern within ourselves and not act on it. Through seva, we not only avoid creating new karma but we burn all the patterns of self-absorption and self-serving that we created in this and past lifetimes.

RECOGNITION: THE FACETS OF OUR SADHANA

It can be useful to think of ourselves as gardeners. What do we choose to grow in our plot of land—despair or unconditional joy? Nobody else chooses for us. A neighbor can throw things over the fence, and their weeds can start to grow in our garden, but they spread and take over only because we don't have the consciousness to identify the weeds and get rid of them.

Some weeds have deep, strong roots and require a lot of effort to dig them out. If we want to completely rid our garden of these intruders, we must dig completely underneath them, lift them out at their source, and then burn the plant. Similarly, with the power of subtle discrimination, we have the capacity to reach below the obvious level of our suffering, to its source. Then we can completely lift out that deeper impurity and burn it in the fire of Consciousness.

There is no real difference between sitting on our cushion and engaging the world, but meditation is where we start. There is a lovely Islamic saying, "Everywhere I look, I see the face of God." This is another way of describing the impression of samadhi. The vision of God's face is right before our eyes because we first saw it in our meditation. Once we are in contact with the Divinity in us, we can repeatedly identify with it until there is no longer any covering of duality.

Shiva is selflessly serving and selflessly receiving. He is completely present as the bliss and joy of Consciousness. Our work—using all of the strategies of the upayas—is to come in contact with our identity as Shiva. He knows who He is. Our capacity to be aware of our state, and therefore to be able to transform it, is this highest Consciousness functioning within us, trying to reveal Itself. Our duty is to allow God to serve His ultimate goal of being free, as us.

Through our sadhana, we each have the power to dissolve all concealment, to reverse the process of forgetting that happened as Shiva's Consciousness moved into condensed form. This sutra powerfully describes sadhana as the conscious choice to find freedom. If we brought as much intensity to reaching God as we apply to everything else in our lives, not allowing anyone or anything to get in the way, we would find our liberation much faster. Every time we tune in to God, we allow for the dissolution of our limited understanding, the dissolution of our ego, and the dissolution of the veils of duality. All this happens by tuning in to the Source from which all duality arose. That is why our meditation is vitally important.

तदा प्रकाशानन्दसारमहामन्त्रवीर्यात्मक-
पूर्णाहन्तावेशात्सदा सर्वसर्गसंहारकारिनिज-
संविद्देवताचक्रेश्वरताप्राप्तिर्भवतीति शिवं

tadā prakāśānandasāramahāmantravīryātamaka-
pūrṇāhantāveshāt sadā sarvasargasaṃhārakārinija-
saṃviddevatācakreśvaratāprāptir bhavatīti śivam

SUTRA TWENTY

Then, for all time—through absorption in the Self, whose nature is the power of the Great Mantra and whose essence is the Bliss of Divine Effulgence one obtains mastery of the wheel of deities (energies) that create and withdraw all that is. This is the auspicious state of Shiva.

Sutra Twenty

Here is the state in which we are complete. There is no experience of separation, no trace of anything but unconditional joy and freedom. Absorbed in the perfection of the Self, beyond the binding that comes from our misunderstanding that we are anything other than That, with every breath, we experience God living as us. How could life be more perfect, when all that is true?

The great mantra, *I am*, is the eternal pulsation and vibration of Consciousness being aware of Itself. Shiva and Shakti, together as Paramashiva, are endlessly repeating, "Aham." That mantra is the breath of life repeating itself over and over again. If my status is the infinite *I am*, and if I created everything out of myself, how could manifestation be anything but perfect? It is up to us to find the subtle discrimination required to recognize this perfection.

The sutra states that one attains mastery of the wheel of deities of Consciousness. In Tantric practices the wheel of deities is understood to be the energy, or power, that emerges from God's absolute Consciousness—and from which all manifest life is created. This is another perspective on the unfolding of existence outlined in the tattvas. There are a number of levels and spheres that function within the wheel of energies. They range from the highest forces that emanate outward to create and eventually reabsorb the entire universe, to the energies that create and sustain all individual existence, including physical bodies and senses.

On the human level we experience the wheel of energies as the vital force that gives us life and awareness. The center of that wheel is our heart, an expression of God's heart that cannot be different or separate from its Source. The heart is our core; it holds the Consciousness and self-reflective capacity of Divine awareness. Emerging out of our heart are the concentric rings of our life. First is the psychic body (the sushumna), the instrument that provides the means to discover and express our consciousness. Then our mind, intellect, physical body, and senses arise—creating the moving chariot of awareness through which we engage our daily life. That action emits another outward circle of energies that form the objects we encounter.

These concentric wheels of deities create the mandala of our experience. Mastery of the wheels happens when we have become Shiva. Being Shiva, we create all manifestation in our life. How amazingly powerful this is! We are the master of all. We recognize our true identity and experience the perfection of our existence.

RECOGNITION: CELEBRATING OUR FREEDOM

Pratyabhijna Hrdayam means the heart of recognition, the heart of Consciousness. Our lives exist for the single purpose of recognizing and celebrating that. If we are the master of all the wheels of creation, the lord of all manifestation, then we dictate our experience of it. We are not a victim of anything. Because we are master of all, we recognize the perfection of life and we surrender to what is. What else can be said?

All this is Shiva. All of manifestation is created in order to conceal Himself, for the joy of recognizing Himself again. "Yes!" is all one can say. We can only affirm, "I am Shiva. I have done all this . . . and in the process I have not forgotten my Self. I have done everything for the pure celebration of freedom."

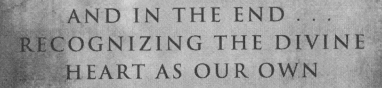

AND IN THE END . . .
RECOGNIZING THE DIVINE
HEART AS OUR OWN

Recognizing the Divine Heart as Our Own

The central message of the *Pratyabhijna Hrdayam* is that liberation happens through the recognition that God dwells within us as our Self. Unconditional joy is the experience that arises from freeing ourselves from our separate identity, from living in duality. These sutras emphatically demonstrate that all suffering comes from our separation from God. Even the other veils of duality—the beliefs that "I am different" and "I am the doer"—are essentially the aftershocks of the experience of being separate from our Source. It is not just the misunderstanding that we are separate but the palpable experience of separation that causes us to suffer.

The *Pratyabhijna Hrdayam* clearly shows us that our experience of life is the result of the choices we make on a moment-to-moment basis. Each individual is free to choose between concealment and revelation, to perpetuate separation or to discover Unity. The sutras go on to describe the practices that reveal our misunderstanding and bring us out of darkness and into the light. This transformation is an experience that completely obliterates our limited perspective and dualistic understanding, and liberation from these forces of concealment is the very purpose of life itself.

All sutras, especially at the time the *Pratyabhijna Hrdayam* was written, were guideposts that said, "Look this way." Before then, the exposition was always passed down by oral transmission.

It was only after the eighth century that Tantrikas decided to preserve this knowledge in the form of scripture, which, in combination with the traditional teacher-student relationship, provided even more powerful means for attaining the highest.

For all of us today these teachings remain an invaluable guide. It is not everyone who feels the longing to know God, which is the arising of Grace in their lives. If you do have that wish for freedom, the only response can be the deepest gratitude for the Grace that has appeared. It is part of that Grace that the wisdom of ancient sages such as Kshemaraja is available to us today to help us on our spiritual journey.

Once you have this knowledge and understand the possibility of attaining unconditional liberation in this life, it is then your choice to free yourself from your limited experience. Although human life is an expression of God's infinite joy, we each choose to conceal or to reveal Divine Consciousness. Don't take the word of anyone, including great saints. Discover the highest in yourself. Exercise the choice to be free.

Throughout this book I have divided the chapters into a discussion of each sutra, followed by a "Recognition" that provides a further explanation of how the text applies to our lives. Similarly, as a conclusion to the book, I'd like to offer a one-year practice that readers can undertake. A great deal of stillness, simplicity, and surrender is required in order to penetrate through the veils of duality. This exercise will help you tune in to that place in yourself.

THE ONE-YEAR PRACTICE: SELFLESSLY SERVING, SELFLESSLY RECEIVING

This practice is a completely internal work, independent from any action you do or do not take in the world. It is designed to help you experience that you are not the doer as you surrender to the Grace that God bestows in every moment of life.

Here are the keys to this yearlong practice:

- Selflessly serve, giving what is wanted without being asked.

- Selflessly receive, accepting what is given, without asking for that which is not.

Let your life show itself to you by surrendering your will to God's will. Find the resonance of the stillpoint that continually repeats, "If it's asked, give it—if it is not given, don't reach for it." You have your life; live it. Be engaged in whatever you are responsible for and do it with depth, joy, and simplicity.

Whenever you are not sure if something is your will or God's will, surrender your will. If there is any struggle about this, it reflects your own misunderstanding. God is crystal clear. If you function from a place of simplicity and stillness, you won't be confused. If there *is* confusion, it is because you haven't gotten still enough inside to see the reality of what is being shown.

When we lack inner stillness, the mantra of doubt starts to resonate in us as an expression of our resistance. This mantra arises from the belief that we need to protect ourselves. We doubt God—and specifically, we doubt God's will for us. So we push back and start to tear apart the threads of our own life. There is nothing more insidious and cancerous than doubt.

So we must ask, "How do I trust?" The answer is simple: Surrender doubt. Trust is inherent within us. When we recognize that we are Shiva we trust our Selves. Shiva never doubts Himself. He knows He's the baddest dude in the land! There is nothing to doubt. In surrendering doubt, we have to let go of all of *our* stuff, all of our misunderstanding, and all of our unwillingness to reach deep inside ourselves and affirm, "*This* is God showing me my life."

As we have discussed, our life has nothing to do with our career or our *this* or our *that*. God only wants you to live from an open heart, because it is only in that place that you will truly experience the bliss and true freedom of being alive. It is only in an open heart that you can celebrate the miracle, the effulgence, and the gift of Grace that gave you life—and the capacity to experience the joy of your own awareness.

THE ESSENCE OF THE ONE-YEAR PRACTICE

The primary instruction can also be stated this way: Don't reach and don't reject. Stop trying to change what you are doing because you think it's necessary in order to feel fulfilled. Whenever the impulse to reach or reject starts to arise, let it go. If any part of you starts questioning and repeating the mantra of stupidity—"What's going to happen to me?"—that is the very part of you to let go of. Whenever an opportunity arises, simply open, be quiet, and don't immediately reach out and grab it. Just open, wait, and surrender even what's being given until it becomes crystal clear that it is a situation that will truly support your growth. If you are not sure, don't do anything. Wait for the clarity.

A lot of what happens in our life is the repetition of karma. Rudi called karma "a shit sandwich" but went on to say that you don't have to take a bite of it! In other words, don't immediately think, "Here is my karma; I must engage with it." Instead, just open, don't do anything, and most of it will just pass on by. If something needs to be dealt with, it will come around again, hit you in the back of the head to get your attention, and then it will slug you in the face. So wait and open, and don't get caught in the form of whatever is happening. Look beneath that to see what is really needed.

Although this yearlong practice is an internal effort, it will happen on the screen of your life. It will show you what it means to surrender the illusion that you are the doer. When you become still, "you" will stop doing. You will start to witness that you are not the doer, because (a) your life will go on, and (b) it just might be a lot more extraordinary than what you would have created if left to your own devices.

Within the day-to-day flow of life we all make hundreds of choices, and that level of activity is not the issue because it is insignificant. Most of these decisions don't have an effect on our state, unless we get caught up in them and project our needs onto everyone and every event. God doesn't really care whether you have granola or Rice Crispies for breakfast. Only you know when you are using your will in a way that prevents God's will from flowing through you.

WALK A YEAR IN GOD'S SHOES

How willing are you to remain still, surrender, and not need anything? Can you surrender every need that comes up and open to whatever life is asking of you in order for you to change? Sit in stillness, and let your life unfold from within you. If you think, "Nothing is unfolding," you are not paying attention to what *is* happening. In other words, if nothing in your day-to-day life changes in the next 365 days, perhaps everything that was truly significant within you *would* change.

Don't wait for your Divine life to show up someday. It is here, right now, as the life you are actually living. If you understand the possibility for transformation inherent in this yearlong challenge, you will be so busy not reaching, and so busy receiving, you won't have time to think about what you did or did not get. If some part of you has to get rearranged in the process of giving what is asked, or stopping your incessant reach, be grateful.

Truly allow the simplicity and the magnificence that is available to you to show itself. The part of you that is afraid to do this is the part of you that will always reinforce the veils of duality. You have to be willing to walk in stillness, in a state where you serve and receive in simplicity, knowing that what is needed is attracted and what is not needed perhaps falls away.

If you can find that place of completeness in yourself and the willingness to surrender, your freedom will show itself. This is not theory. This is isn't what somebody else does. This isn't what we do after we are free. This is what we do to *become* free.

We need to pay attention to whatever is trying to change us, to reveal that we are already complete as we are. Look at the dynamics that are requiring you to open up and get bigger—or requiring that you let go, so that you can get bigger. Nityananda said, "Surrender everything that keeps you separate from Shiva." Believing that we are the doer is the field upon which we act out all of our limited impulses. I encourage you to surrender being the doer, because this is the only way to understand that your life is not about you—it's about living as the expression of God.

When most of us think about Unity, what we are really doing is trying to understand duality and how it works. So do this: Stop trying to understand duality. Reach for Unity. You cannot understand the experience of Oneness through a dualistic experience. The veils of separation and differentiation, of thinking, "I am the agent," are very powerful. They contain the energy behind the transmigration of our soul.

If we understand that it is the arresting of that transmigration that frees us, then why would we be so concerned about not being the doer? Why should we worry about trying to figure out the nature of our separation? Those concerns are the very things to surrender. We only need to expose dualistic consciousness within ourselves so that the effects of those boundaries have less capacity to trap our consciousness and lock us in a limited dimension.

This is your work. The consciousness that you have to bring to it has many levels, both in your internal practice and in your engagement with your day-to-day life. You don't stop meditating or stop your normal activities, but you must focus on doing all of that from a place of surrendering your will.

See what happens. And if, a few months down the road, you think nothing has happened, find a deeper stillness. Look for a change in your internal experience instead of a change in your life. Your understanding of "I am not the doer" should have deeply penetrated within you.

There's a term called *Bhairava Mudra*, which means "external gaze, internal focus." We are engaged in seeing the world, while our focus is inside. See what the world shows you, but understand it from within. It requires a continuous gaze to see what the Divine will is for you in each situation. Allow your consciousness to be changed by stopping the incessant need to change everything. Maybe life is perfect the way it is. By not engaging the part of you that needs to change it, you will see the perfection in what actually exists.

Seeing life with this clarity, without feeling the need to change anything, requires a great surrendering of will. We must let go, again and again, and let God's will show itself. That's why it's said that the highest action is non-action. We are still doing, but from a place of stillness and selfless service—from a state of surrender that allows God to live as us. If you are not sure whether you are supposed to do something, don't do anything. If you are not sure after you've asked ten times, try the eleventh.

I am suggesting some very explicit work for the next year, a powerful practice that will awaken your own heart. It will transmute your experience of duality—bringing you to the recognition of the Unity of all life and the unwavering awareness that God lives as you. Selflessly serving and selflessly receiving is living from stillness and profound surrender. This is the doorway into liberation. There is no greater treasure than your own heart, for that is where you will recognize your Divinity.

It is your choice to live from the recognition that you are Shiva, and you are free.

The Double-Breath Exercise

The double-breath exercise is an important tool for meditation. It will help you to experience and deepen the flow of vital force. It's an integration of our wish to grow and of the awareness of the breath, the chakras, and the flow into one smooth process. Do the double-breath every ten minutes during meditation to sharpen your inner focus. Use it throughout the day.

DOING THE EXERCISE

- Take a deep breath, let it go, and relax.

- Be aware that the breath is filled with spiritual energy and nourishment.

- Draw the next breath into the heart chakra. As the breath moves through the throat chakra, swallow. Allow the breath to fill and open your chest, but do not force the breath. Relax in the heart chakra and feel an expansion taking place. Feel a deep wish to grow. Ask deeply to open your heart; ask deeply to surrender your worries, problems and boundaries. Hold the breath in the heart for about ten seconds or until it naturally releases. Release about one-fifth of the breath, deeply let go—keep your attention and the energy in your heart.

- Breathe in again, through the heart, bringing the breath and your attention into your navel/abdominal chakra. Hold gently and relax deeply, feel your belly open and soften with the expansion of energy. Hold the breath and your attention there for about ten seconds. As you release the breath feel the energy naturally expand across the sex chakra and into the base of the spine.

- Relax the base of the spine and allow the energy to rise up the spinal column to the top of the head. Feel the energy there.

- At other times during meditation remain very aware of your breath—at the end of each outbreath, let go, and then let go again. Feel the expansion in yourself. Surrender inside, allowing something deeper and finer to fill you.

With the double-breath you are working to establish a flow of energy down the front and up the back. When not doing the double-breath, focus your breath and attention on the heart chakra and be aware of the flow of energy moving down through the chakras and up the spinal column to the top of the head. It is this ever-deepening practice that mobilizes your inner energy to facilitate a very profound and lasting change in your consciousness and in your experience in life.

****

Aham Mantra Meditation

A free MP3 download of a guided meditation with the Aham mantra by Swami Khecaranatha is available to those who have purchased this book. Please go to *TrikaShala.com* and open the Writings & Photos page from the left-side menu. Then click on the Guided Meditation link under Swami Khecaranatha's name. When prompted, enter the password AHM7 (all caps). This will take you to a page with the MP3 file.

About the Author

Swami Khecaranatha has practiced and taught Kundalini MahaYoga since 1972. With a mastery derived from four decades of dedicated inner practice and selfless service, he is an authentic adept of Tantric Shaivism and an initiated lineage carrier in the shaktipat tradition of Bhagavan Nityananda and Swami Rudrananda (Rudi). Based on the profound spiritual transformation he experienced in his own life through the practice of Kundalini Yoga and the Grace of his teachers, he offers inspirational and practical guidance that can change a reader's life as well.

Khecaranatha was born in 1951 in Illinois to an American family in circumstances comparable to those of most of his readers. His own life has demonstrated that it is possible to live fully in the world while developing and maintaining one's conscious connection to the Divinity within. After meeting his teacher Rudi in 1971, he moved into Rudi's ashram in Indiana, and Rudi recognized him as a teacher within this lineage in 1972. After Rudi took *mahasamadhi* in 1973, Khecaranatha continued to work with Swami Chetanananda, the spiritual leader of the ashram, and lived as a member of that community as it subsequently moved to Cambridge, Massachusetts, and finally to Portland, Oregon.

Serving as the head teacher under Chetanananda, he was, through the years, instrumental in helping to develop the ashrams that Rudi had started. While living in an ashram for thirty years he also held several "real-world" jobs, including that of CEO of a multimillion-dollar consulting business. This personal experience has strengthened his conviction that there is no separation between spiritual life and life in the world. In 2001 Khecaranatha moved to Berkeley, California, to start a spiritual center, called Sacred Space Yoga Sanctuary. Sacred Space offers in-depth instruction in Kundalini Yoga (the TrikaShala program) and immersions into Trika Shaivism. In addition to teaching, Swami Khecaranatha currently serves as director of Rudramandir: A Center for Spirituality and Healing, which is operated by Sacred Space.

Rudi, Khecaranatha's "root guru," called his practice "the work." He developed a powerful set of techniques, including a unique "open-eyes class" for giving shaktipat, an integral part of Kundalini MahaYoga. Although he did not study scripture, Rudi's practice and teachings were a perfect expression of the most sacred of the Tantric Shaivite practices of ancient times. While Rudi had several teachers, it was his relationship with Bhagavan Nityananda that catapulted his growth to its most profound dimensions. Although he only met Nityananda a few times before the saint's passing, Rudi described this profound relationship as existing on a spiritual level that was not limited by the absence of Nityananda's physical form.

Nityananda, whose name means "Bliss of the eternal," was a holy person who was considered an *avadhut*, a direct link to the Absolute. He lived in southwestern India from around the turn of the twentieth century until 1961. By the late 1930s he was established in Ganeshpuri, a small village in the countryside near Mumbai, where his presence attracted thousands of people and an active ashram developed around him. The essence of his teaching was that liberation occurs within every person when they merge their own individual consciousness into the Divine, and Nityananda emphasized the awakening of the Kundalini as the path to liberation. In India today he continues to be revered as a great saint.

In July of 2002 Khecaranatha took formal vows of *sannyas* and was initiated into the Saraswati Order by Ma Yoga Shakti, a swami who lives in New York. He was given the name Swami Khecaranatha, which means "Moving in the fullness of the Divine Heart." A swami, or *sannyasin,* is unconditionally committed to serve, love, and support other people in their spiritual growth. To fulfill that undertaking, Khecaranatha continues to teach and to serve as the spiritual leader of a community of practitioners at TrikaShala.

Other books by Swami Khecaranatha include *Depth Over Time: Kundalini MahaYoga, A Path of Transformation and Liberation,* and *Merging With the Divine, One Day at a Time.* More information about his practice, books, and guided-meditation CDs can be found at *SwamiKhecaranatha.com.*

TrikaShala

Swami Khecaranatha is the spiritual leader of TrikaShala, the meditation program of Sacred Space Yoga Sanctuary, a nonprofit organization in Berkeley, California. TrikaShala teaches Kundalini Meditation through classes, retreats, immersions, and engagement with a spiritual community. Weekly classes, which include shaktipat transmission, are free of charge. For more information about attending your first Kundalini class or retreat, please call (510) 486-8700 or visit *TrikaShala.com*.

Rudramandir

TrikaShala is located in Rudramandir: A Center for Spirituality and Healing. Its mission is to serve the community by offering a breadth of programs to aid in the exploration of each individual's full potential. The experience of celebration and expansion at Rudramandir is enhanced through the adornment of the space with sacred art in the form of sculpture, painting, and architectural elements, evoking the magnificence of Spirit. Additional information is available at *Rudramandir.com*.

Made in the USA
Middletown, DE
13 October 2023

40758634R00172